LIFE IN THE SPIRIT

LIFE IN THE SPIRIT

Christian Holiness in Doctrine, Experience, and Life

by
RICHARD S. TAYLOR

Approved Christian Service Training Text
for Unit 115b, "Bible Holiness"

BEACON HILL PRESS
Kansas City, Missouri

Copyright 1966 by
Beacon Hill Press

First Printing, 1966

Printed in the United States of America

Foreword

The publication of any book that assists toward a correct understanding of the Word of God in any area is an estimable project. But when such a production is concerned with the subject of Bible holiness, it is of more than ordinary significance.

Furthermore, when such a Bible study guide is directed particularly toward a better understanding of the doctrine of holiness by laymen, the possibilities for greater knowledge of divine truth and for enrichment of spiritual experience are broad and especially meaningful.

However, the essential value of such a publication is in its authorship, and at this point this book possesses an eminent quality. Dr. Richard Taylor, presently associate professor of theology at Nazarene Theological Seminary, has had a successful career as preacher, teacher, author, and college administrator. But in relation to this book it is of special importance that through the years he has gained a well-deserved reputation for competence in the area of scriptural holiness and the experience of entire sanctification. Thus our people can be assured of the orthodoxy and correctness of this guide.

The Christian Service Training leadership is to be commended for the commissioning and distribution of this book and the promotion of the course of study which it serves.

I recommend this publication to holiness people everywhere with the sincere hope that many thousands will avail themselves of the opportunity offered for gaining new insights into the Word of God, and for the strengthening of vital Christian faith.

—HUGH C. BENNER
General Superintendent
Church of the Nazarene

Preface

One is tempted to wish that the twelve chapters of this book could be expanded to a "baker's dozen," for there are several important topics yet left over which might be thrown together in an added chapter. For instance, Discipline in the Spirit-filled Life, Praying in the Spirit, Knowing the Word, How to Handle Depression, The Art of Public and Private Testimony are just a few of the topics begging for discussion. But in attempting to give a comprehensive and practical survey of the most basic phases of *Life in the Spirit*, some subjects must of necessity be bypassed and some questions left untouched. It is hoped that the book as it is, in spite of its shortcomings, will aid many sincere and honest Christians in coming, not only to a clear understanding of the doctrine, but above all into the happy enjoyment of the blessing of the fullness of the Spirit. It is hoped also that the study of this volume will prompt further reading in the books listed at the end of the last chapter.

I wish to acknowledge with deep appreciation my indebtedness to Rev. Bennett Dudney, Christian Service Training director, and Dr. J. Fred Parker, book editor, for their valuable counsel and guidance in the preparation of this book. I am grateful also to Mr. Jerry McCant for his assistance in checking details, and certainly to Miss Betty Fuhrman, who typed the final copy.

The titles of the chapters will reveal that the book falls naturally into two divisions. The first six chapters explain the biblical doctrine of heart holiness and seek to show the way into the experience. The second six chapters describe the privileges, responsibilities, and also the limitations of the Spirit-filled life. Therefore, though it was prepared as a "Series b" C.S.T. text, it could be used in two separate six-week courses (though possibly the C.S.T. Commission should not be told that I have the temerity to make the suggestion).

RICHARD S. TAYLOR

Acknowledgments

Scripture quotations from special versions of the Bible have been used herein as follows:

New American Standard Bible. Copyright 1960, 1962, 1963, by the Lockman Foundation, La Habra, California.

The New English Bible. © The Delegates of the Oxford University Press and the Syndics of the Cambridge University Press, 1961.

The New Testament in Modern English. © J. B. Phillips, 1958. Used by permission of the Macmillan Company.

Revised Standard Version of the Holy Bible. Copyrighted 1946 and 1952 by the Division of Christian Education of the National Council of Churches.

Permission has also been granted to quote from *Living Letters,* by Ken Taylor, published by the Grason Company, Minneapolis, Minnesota.

Contents

1. What God Requires 11
2. The Christian's Failure 29
3. In Search for the Cause 42
4. The Divine Provision 56
5. The Divine Plan of Realization 76
6. The Faith That Sanctifies 91
7. A Life of Power 109
8. The Guidance of the Spirit 125
9. The Humanity of the Sanctified 149
10. The Ethics of Holiness—Biblical Principles .. 169
11. The Ethics of Holiness—Some Problem Areas .. 186
12. Turning Temptation into Triumph 204

CHAPTER ONE

What God Requires

Scriptures for background:

On holiness: Luke 1:67-75; Heb. 12:12-17; I Pet. 1:13-22. On love: Luke 10:25-37; Rom. 13:8-10; I Cor. 13:1-13; I John 4:16-21. Plus the Sermon on the Mount, Matthew 5; 6; 7.

A store clerk leaned over the counter and earnestly asked J. G. Morrison this question: "Brother Morrison, how little religion can a man have and still get to heaven?" Before considering the preacher's answer, look squarely at the question itself. It discloses a desire to find the lowest level of religious attainment that is consistent with safety. In the heart of the inquirer is a basic aversion to spiritual things; his religion is for him a necessary nuisance as a means of avoiding hell; it is about as palatable as the costly insurance on his home and car which he carries grudgingly. He may not have analyzed his own heart, but actually he is a double-cheat, for he is scheming to cheat both God and the devil. He wants God's salvation without serving Him with all his heart; thus he cheats God out of the full measure of devotion due Him. At the same time he wants enough religion to cheat the devil out of his soul in the end.

The preacher looked at his questioner in his piercing way and replied: "Just enough to make him comfortable in the presence of Jesus." One look at Calvary, and the Man on the middle cross, hanging there in shame for our redemption, will quickly convince us that no one could be comfortable in His presence who despised His blood and resented His lordship as an annoying intrusion into one's personal liberty.

Yet, having scorned the clerk's question, we must hasten to say that in any honest effort to study the Bible doctrine of salvation this is the very question, in essence, which we must ask. What is the level of grace which God has provided for us, and will *require* of all who have light and opportunity as an inviolable condition for final salvation? No more important question could be asked.

But our attitude must differ from that of the store clerk or we will be doomed to confusion before we start. Our inquiry must not be prompted by a desire to learn how little we can get by with (and having learned that will strive for no more); rather it must be an honest desire to know God's full will for us, that we might attain unto it. This axiom we can lay down at the outset: *The minimum measure of grace acceptable would be an intense desire for the maximum measure of grace available.*

It is in this spirit that we approach this study. In this first chapter we shall go directly to the Bible to discover exactly what God does require. We do not desire to cheapen the standard of Christian life and experience by lowering it unscripturally. But neither do we wish to exaggerate it. In one direction is an easy optimism which sees little need for the atoning Blood. In the other direction are discouragement and despair—or even worse, a callous presumption that, since we can't help our failures, the responsibility for somehow "getting us through" is God's. Of course, in the latter case, it is useless to lose any sleep over our sins, as long as we are "Christians" and live a reasonably decent and religious life.

We shall find that an honest study of God's Word affords little comfort for either the easy optimist or the careless Christian. In fact we may as well affirm at the outset that the death and resurrection of our Lord were intended not only to atone for man's past sinful failures, but to bring an *end* to such failure by making him truly and triumphantly what God requires him to be. Jesus did not die to make holiness unnecessary, but to make it possible. Which leads us to our first tenet:

HOLINESS IS REQUIRED

Holiness is not an option. No matter how many times he has heard Heb. 12:14 the student who takes the Bible seriously can never escape being jolted by the flat ultimatum that without holiness "no man shall see the Lord."[1] But this ultimatum is repeated over and over in different forms. In Rom. 6:19, Paul sees "everlasting life" as the legitimate "end" of that "fruit unto holiness" which characterizes him who has been made "free from sin," as a servant to God. It is not without reason that in II Cor. 7:1, where Paul urges the Corinthian believers to purge themselves from "all filthiness of the flesh and spirit, perfecting holiness," he adds "in the fear of the Lord." It is perilous not to! For he has just reminded them (in chapter 6) that their sonship absolutely depends on separating themselves from all ungodliness. The unclean thing is not even to be "touched."

[1] It is important to understand (and any student of the Greek text will confirm this) that "seeing the Lord" is not dependent on achieving peace with all men, but only on the possession of holiness. As valuable and desirable as is harmony with men, it is not of supreme importance; there is something even greater.

To the Thessalonians he writes that he who despises God's call to holiness "despiseth not man, but God" (I Thess. 4:8). He also links holiness with the Second Coming as the proper and essential preparation for that great event (I Thess. 3:13; 5:23). But Paul is not alone in this, for Peter does the same thing: "Seeing then that all these things shall be dissolved, what manner of persons ought ye to be in all holy conversation [living] and godliness?" (II Pet. 3:11) Even more forceful is 3:14: "Wherefore, beloved, seeing that ye look for such things, be diligent that ye may be found of him in peace, without spot, and blameless."

But the somberness of the ultimatum reaches its climax in the words of John the Revelator: "He that is unjust, let him be unjust still: and he which is filthy, let him be filthy still: and he that is righteous, let him be righteous still: and he that is holy, let him be holy still" (Rev. 22:11). Coming as they do in the last chapter of the Bible, these words are sobering indeed. As a mighty bell they toll the verdict of divine justice on the destiny of immortal souls. Righteousness and holiness are placed over against unjustness and filthiness. The first two words mark the character of the saved, the last two the character of the lost. And thus the Bible solemnly closes with this epitome of the basic moral principle permeating all of its pages: God requires holiness in men as a condition for eternal fellowship with himself.[2]

---

[2]The Bible nowhere affirms that without tongues, or miracles, or other signs and wonders, no man shall see the Lord. Holiness alone is the one indispensable for heaven, and holiness is a quality of *being*. That such holiness has its source in the merit of the Blood and the power of the Spirit, received by faith, is of course assumed; there is no hint here of *self*-righteousness or self-attained holiness. But it also is affirmed that "faith" which does not lead to genuine holiness is sub-Christian, and *thwarts* the real purpose of both the Blood and the Spirit. As such it is a covert form of unbelief rather than faith.

His cause. Perfect love excludes even the possibility of hypocrisy, with its secret covetousness and stinginess, which pinches pennies with God but is lavish with self— fine cars, soft carpets, elite meals, and "first class" trips, but extreme caution and "prudence" on Sunday when the offering plate is passed. But *life itself* is zealously devoted, not just money. The voice, talents, ambitions, affections—all are made to serve. Whatever cannot serve is discarded as superfluous baggage (Heb. 12:1).

Love expels fear. Such perfect love casts out fear (I John 4:17-18). It does not eliminate all spontaneous fear of physical danger, such as the impulse to hide from a tornado, nor does it exclude "the fear of the Lord" which "is the beginning of wisdom" (Prov. 9:10; Acts 5:11). But it expels the fear "which hath torment." This is fear which arises in contemplating the judgment. In other words, it is an inner anxiety of the soul, a nagging uneasiness concerning our true relationship with God. But such fear is impossible in the happy glow of perfect submission and perfect trust. "There is no fear in love." We say with Paul, "I know whom I have believed, and am persuaded that he is able to keep that which I have committed unto him against that day" (II Tim. 1:12). Obedience to the first commandment therefore is not consistent with ceaseless and disabling anxieties. A fretful, peevish, worrying spirit indicts our love for God as defective.

PERFECT LOVE TOWARD MEN

But as we return to the Scriptures we discover that God's requirement is yet more extensive. We are commanded to love men as well as God. When men are shut out, God is shut out too, "for he that loveth not his brother whom he hath seen, how can he love God whom he hath not seen?" (I John 4:20) Therefore we cannot choose to obey only one of the great commandments.

We obey both or neither. In the same breath that Jesus enunciates the first commandment, He adds, "and thy neighbour as thyself" (Luke 10:27). This is the "second" (Matt. 22:39), which, though distinguishable from the first, is inseparable from it. What does it mean? It is not difficult to understand, as a simple analysis will show.

The object of love: the neighbor. Rather gleefully the lawyer shot back: "And who is my neighbour?" In his mind the definition was narrow and exclusive. But Jesus told the simple and heartwarming story of the Good Samaritan. When He had finished He turned to His interrogator and neatly turned the question around: "Which now of these three, thinkest thou, was neighbour unto him that fell among the thieves?" He is saying: You have asked the wrong question, a question that true love never asks. The right question is, "To whom may I be a neighbor?" Love does not seek to exclude but to include. The right question has but one right answer: Love puts within me a neighborly heart that knows no barriers of race or color, but sees my neighbor as anyone who needs me, and who is providentially called to my attention.

When in the Sermon on the Mount Jesus warned that "except your righteousness shall exceed the righteousness of the scribes and Pharisees, ye shall in no case enter into the kingdom of heaven," He had exactly this sort of thing in mind (Matt. 5:20-48). For the Pharisees not only lived under the *lex talionis* ("an eye for an eye, and a tooth for a tooth"—exact retribution) but also under the principle of *reciprocity* ("you scratch my back and I'll scratch yours"). In this spirit the term "neighbor" was a label reserved for the very few. Its definition was circumscribed by all sorts of lines and qualifications. But Jesus cancelled utterly this philosophy of life by the command: "Be ye therefore perfect, even as your Father which is in heaven is perfect." He meant that as the love of God was all-inclusive so must ours be. The enemy, the ugly and unlovely, the wretch who can give nothing in return, the stranger and the "foreigner," the man of a different color, race, or nationality—all are the proper objects of this love which is required in the second commandment.

The kind of love required: "agape." This is the English spelling of the Greek word used in both commandments, and used generally in the New Testament with a distinctively Christian meaning. It is Godlike love, which transcends purely social considerations of obligation or attraction. It sees farther and deeper than human love; it perceives spiritual needs and eternal issues; it sees men in the light of the judgment, and seeing, it seeks the highest welfare of all.

Will Rogers said, "I never saw a man I didn't like." That is *philia,* a human liking for people, which is referred to a few times in the New Testament. It is a love between equals. It is warmth of mutual attraction. We "like" some people without half trying; it requires no "grace" to do so. What Will Rogers referred to was only *philia;* the Christian must have *agape.* Its magnetic pole is not self but Christ, and through Him our fellowmen. We are blessed too on the rebound, but the dynamic of love is not selfishness but honest interest *outward.* When William Booth was unable to attend a great gathering of the Salvation Army in New York City he was asked to send a message by cable. It was the single word "Others." That is meaningless sentimentalism to the one who knows nothing of *agape* love. Yet this is the very kind of love by which we must be possessed. Let us not prematurely throw up our hands and exclaim, "How?" It is our purpose now to discover only the *what* of God's requirement.

The measure of love required: as ourselves. We are in difficulty here unless we see that the love required of us is not measured in terms of how *much* we love ourselves but in the *manner* in which we love ourselves.

No one knows how much he loves himself. To try to fix an exact degree, in order that we might know how much we must love our neighbor, would introduce a new legalism. Love would once again be corroded by the acid of bargaining. When love starts bargaining for so much and no more, it ceases to be love. It is seeking for a loophole, a way out. If we knew exactly how much was our duty to love, and could say, "Now I have loved all I need to; it's someone else's turn," we would betray the fact that selfishness, not love, lay at the core of our lives after all. Let us not then inject a new legalism by interpreting this measure of love to be a measure of *degree*.

But when we ask, *"How* do I love myself?" we immediately have a handle we can get hold of. How do we love? We *respect* ourselves (or *should,* by dressing and conducting ourselves as ladies and gentlemen). We *protect* ourselves from cold and hunger and poverty and danger. We *provide* for ourselves, as the ant who works in summer to prepare for winter, in contrast to the sluggard. We *preserve* ourselves from disease and untimely death by getting proper food and rest (and by careful driving). If we are wise we will work even harder to preserve our good name and our influence. We will seek our *highest welfare* above all, which means the salvation of our souls and the establishment of strong Christian character. In all these ways it is proper and right to love ourselves.

Now, Jesus is saying: "Start doing exactly the same thing to people around you. Respect them too. Protect, provide for, preserve them also. Seek their highest welfare—be concerned about the salvation of others just as sincerely as you are about your own salvation." This will involve us in the stream of human life. We will bear in our hearts perpetual concern about human injustice and degradation, wherever found and by whomsoever suffered. *Agape* love seeks the *highest* welfare of others;

therefore when it touches them it will not tarnish them. Their good name, their influence, their character, their happiness, their health and prosperity will be our concern always. The more we love ourselves in these ways, the more will we love others. Such love will never gloat over the sins of others. It will not lay temptation in their way, by carelessness in dress or behavior, as did Potiphar's wife. It will not inveigle them into any compromise with conscience. It will not engage in any business which exploits the vices and weaknesses of men.

This is loving as we love ourselves. Rather than the gospel emphasis being on exact degree, and thus a new form of legalism, the gospel emphasis moves in the opposite direction. An imbalance in favor of the other person is gradually evolved as a sort of inner-circle standard or privilege. John the Baptist gladly said, "He must increase, but I must decrease" (John 3:30). Paul said, "I could wish that myself were accursed from Christ for my brethren" (Rom. 9:3). And Jesus voiced this superlative love in these quiet words in the Upper Room: "Greater love hath no man than this, that a man lay down his life for his friends" (John 15:13). That's crowding self out! This may not be a requirement for salvation. But to launch out on the path that *is* required is dangerous to self-interest, for *agape* love has a way of taking over, and elbowing self farther and farther into the corner. In fact, Christian love never feels that it has fully discharged its duty to others; in its zeal to do so it becomes less and less anxious about what happens to self. If self at times seems to be protected, it is only that others may be served the more.

A Limited Requirement

That love is the focal point of the divine requirement as presented in the Scriptures there can be no doubt. The two great commandments faithfully represent the whole. They are not inconsequential molehills which have been blown up out of due proportion. Rather they are our Lord's own verdict on the subject of comparative truth. They also reflect the emphasis of every New Testament writer, each in his own way, but in unmistakable parallel.[6]

If love is basic, it is wise to ask what the relationship is between love and holiness. These two terms cannot be fully defined apart from each other. Holiness is the state of love in the heart and the practice of love in the life. It is more: it is a state of inner soundness in which such love has been made natural and has been established as the norm. Thus there is no confusion of outward lip-service to love and its absence in the heart. There is no Christian holiness without love, and there is no Christian love apart from holiness. Paul put it this way: "The aim and object of this command is the love which springs from a clean heart, from a good conscience, and from faith that is genuine" (I Tim. 1:5, NEB). Total all that up and we get holiness. Erase a single factor and holiness is destroyed.

A quality of spirit. If such *love-holiness* is God's requirement, it is necessary to inquire as to the nature of its boundaries. It is essentially a quality of man's spirit and the direction of his life. It is that within a man which *structures* his character, his choices, his standard of values, his goals and aims. As such, the requirement as to quality is absolute. Any spirit or motivation con-

---

[6]The New Testament presents love as the *touchstone* of all other standards and values.

    a. *Of righteousness*—Matt. 22:40; Rom. 13:8-10; II Cor. 5:14-15; Titus 2:11-14; Jas. 2:14-17.

    b. *Of service*—I Cor. 13:3.

    c. *Of worship*—John 4:24; Matt. 5:23-24.

    d. *Of Christian character*—Col. 3:12-14; I Corinthians 13.

trary to love spoils its perfection, and is sin before God. It must be:

1. A love that is *morally sound,* which excludes illicit lust and greed in all their forms.

2. A love that is *religiously pure,* which excludes double-mindedness in God's sight in our basic motivation and allegiance (Jas. 4:8).

3. A love that is *materially practical,* which impels faithful stewardship and deeds of benevolence or "good works" (I John 3:17).

4. A love that is *socially universal,* which includes all men, the enemy and outcast as well as the friend, and has no room for either snobbery or vindictiveness.

Imperfect in expression. But having insisted on its absoluteness as the governing quality of our being, we must just as energetically affirm that nowhere in the Bible are we given license to measure love by the yardstick of its perfect expression. For the expression of love at once involves other factors besides love. To attempt to express love brings into play our knowledge and our judgment, and even our material resources. Both the need and our love may dictate a gift of money, but it is highly probable that we may not have as much as both need and love require. Furthermore, there is not the slightest indication that God requires of us either perfect knowledge or perfect judgment; yet there cannot be perfect expression of love without them. Love seeks to win a soul, but doesn't always know how; in its very zeal it may drive away rather than win. Love seeks to be fair, but judgment in all honesty may pronounce a verdict that proves unfair—which requires amends in the form of apology and self-humbling. Did love fail? No, only judgment.

Imperfect in degree. Again, we need to repeat that perfect love is not perfection of *degree;* that is, it is not so strong and full-orbed that there is no possibility of development. Love may be *pure,* yet grow in *strength.* (Ask any happy golden wedding celebrants!) So also confirms the Scripture: I Thess. 4:9-10.

Not equally expressed to all. Furthermore, scriptural love does not cancel or abrogate certain God-ordained priorities in the areas of human affection and duty. Though we may love the neighbors with a love that is divine and genuine, it is still true that we are to love our companions and our children in a way that we are not required to love the neighbors. A Christian family may be specifically led by the Holy Spirit to sacrifice its security in behalf of others; but this does not abrogate I Tim. 5:8 as the *norm,* nor does it cancel the special and different quality of affection we feel for our own. Even Jesus apparently loved some with special tenderness and affection.

Then, we have a special duty to the Church: "As we have therefore opportunity, let us do good unto all men, especially unto them who are of the household of faith" (Gal. 6:10).

It is necessary to see these biblical limitations lest we dash off with groundless inferences above love's impossibility and impracticability; or lest we be infected with a basic Calvinistic and Lutheran error: that God's requirements are so high that we cannot keep them *even with grace.* Obviously, what He does require is impossible *without* grace; but to say the standard is so high that God must help men is not the same as to say that it is so high that even God's help is not enough.

Could it be that such erroneous thinking arises out of a misapprehension of the true biblical standard? To lower the standard beneath the biblical norm to the point where any man of reasonably good will could attain to it easily would be to reduce Christianity to humanism and cancel any real need for the grace of God. But to raise the standard unreasonably high—above a sound interpretation of Scripture—is to involve God in contradiction, injustice, and failure. This would mean that even the cross of Christ plus the power of the Spirit is not quite sufficient to enable the child of God to be what God demands he shall be—*thoroughly good.* Thus the scheme of redemption includes an element of failure and is salvaged only by theological juggling.

SUMMARY

1. In our inquiry into God's requirements we have found that God demands holiness of men, consisting of inward soundness and outward righteousness, with love constituting its dynamic force and its central quality.

2. This love must be perfect toward God in the sense of the total devotion of the whole man. All basic disloyalties must be dislodged from the heart. The Psalmist's prayer, "Unite my heart to fear thy name" (Ps. 86:11), must be answered.

3. It must also flow toward others, with regard to need, but without regard to social standing or race. We are to love, not just as much as we love ourselves, but in the various ways we love ourselves. This love is dynamic. It is compulsive. It is more than sentimental feeling; it is practical action.

4. It is a love which increasingly subordinates self in the exciting quest of the welfare and happiness of others. In the end it finds that making others happy makes self happy too. But even this fact will short-circuit true love if it gets in the way by occupying the focus of our attention. If we are good to others just so they will be good to us, we are being motivated just as truly by selfishness as the person who is deliberately mean to others.

5. But it is a love which, while perfect, has its limitations. It is not as strong as it shall be if pursued by divine grace. It does not cancel special obligations to family and church—or even community and nation.

6. God's requirement is thus seen to focus in man's attitudes and relationships, rather than in intellectual understanding or skillful performance. This fact will help us to understand what *sin* is in God's sight, and what constitutes *failure*.

QUESTIONS FOR DISCUSSION

1. How can we love God with *all* the heart, etc., and still love friends and loved ones?

2. What is the "love of the world" which is incompatible with the "love of the Father" (I John 2:15)?

3. Which is more seriously detrimental—to interpret the Bible as presenting an impossible standard (even with the aid of grace) or as presenting an easy standard which can be reached without much grace?

CHAPTER TWO

The Christian's Failure

Scriptures for background:

Matt. 16:13-24; 25:1-46; Mark 9:33-41; Luke 22:24-34; I Cor. 3:1-4; Heb. 5:11—6:2; Jas. 3:6—4:8

As offensive as the word "failure" may be, it compels us to examine subnormal Christian living in the light of the biblical standard. The question is often asked, "Can a Christian who is born again but not yet sanctified wholly live a completely victorious life?" For the moment the answer must be *yes* and *no*. Obviously a lack of victory is failure, and failure is lack of victory. But neither failure nor victory can be defined without referral to the *standard*. Any "victory" must be in terms of measurable goals. In religion, if the standard is set low enough, the answer can be an easy yes (with a chuckle). Even a good-natured heathen could live such a "victorious life." But if the standard is set too high, and defined as absolute perfection in performance as well as in heart, then *all* of us fail, not only the justified but the sanctified too.

Furthermore, we would have to consign all Christians to perpetual failure if the standard which they were failing to reach was their full potential in spiritual stature. If we think of what God *plans* for us, and has provided in His grace, in the sense of maturity and depth and skill, we are always behind. But the question is, Are we merely behind what God expects us to be *next year,* or are we also behind in what He expects of us today? The contractor who hasn't yet finished the house because he has six more weeks in the contract can't be accused of failing, even though the house is incomplete. But if he is *behind schedule,* and not catching up, he is in a serious bind, and something needs to be done fast. This was the predicament of the Hebrew Christians: "For indeed, though by this time you ought to be teachers, you need someone to teach you the ABC of God's oracles over again" (Heb. 5:12, NEB). This was retrogression, not progress. Walking behind light always spells failure in some measure, and if continued will soon bring disaster.

The question then is still with us: Is it proper to speak about "failure" in the Christian life, and can an unsanctified child of God fully avoid failure of sufficient seriousness to plague him and shame him?

No Dual Standard ...

Perhaps this is the right time to puncture a very popular fallacy. It is the supposition that God doesn't expect as much of Christians not yet in the full blessing of holiness. That there is a smidgin of truth in this doesn't compensate for the dangerous delusion. No one expects a *learner* to operate a car as skillfully as a veteran driver, but that does not mean that there are two sets of laws, one for the beginner and one for the veteran. There are not two standards of driving. The rules of the road apply to both equally, and both are committed to the same standard: *safe driving.* Similarly

God doesn't suddenly "up" the requirements the moment a believer is made holy in heart. There is only one standard for angels, demons, and men: *holiness*. God requires that all moral agents love Him supremely and obey Him implicitly. Their failure is what makes them backsliders, sinners, or demons—or defeated Christians who must flee to the Blood to avoid one of the three categories.

An enthusiastic convert, zealous in personal work and church activities, explained to me in all earnestness that he didn't dare seek entire sanctification, for that would necessitate altering some of his business methods! He wanted to be holy, but not *that* holy. But it was hastily explained to him that if his business methods were questionable in his own mind they were wrong for him as a *Christian*. Avoiding entire sanctification for himself would not sanctify them!

The truth is that all Christians are committed to a life of holiness. This much is implied in repentance. J. A. Wood says: "If a man is a Christian, and in a justified state, he has the heart of a child of God and desires to render Him a *present, full* and *unreserved* obedience. A desire for holiness is a spontaneity of the regenerate heart."[1] When the opposite temper, an *aversion to holiness,* has gotten the upper hand, the person is a backslider—or is at least on the way.

Now we are ready to be more exact in our "yes and no" answer, and in so doing get off the fence. The standard by which a Christian's victory or failure is to be measured is holiness of heart and life, defined in terms of perfect love to God and man. This is the Bible standard, as we discovered in the first chapter.

1. Any Christian can certainly live "victoriously," from the moment of conversion, in the sense of main-

---

[1] J. A. Wood, *Perfect Love* (Chicago: The Christian Witness Co., 1880), p. 29.

taining his purpose to live for God and his commitment to holiness in principle. But of course this means "walking in all the light," which includes the light on entire sanctification.

2. Any Christian can also live victoriously in the sense that he can (and must) avoid the *practice* of known sin. He must make no allowance for sin in his planning. He clings to nothing which he perceives to be wrong. He is honest in searching the Scriptures and listening to preaching that he might know what belongs to the Christian life and what does not. He can resolutely refuse through regenerating grace to be the dog that turns "to his own vomit again," or the "sow that was washed to her wallowing in the mire" (II Pet. 2:22). This kind of "victorious living" is demanded by the very nature of sonship as explained in I John 3:4-10. But this too implies *obedience* to the light of sanctification.

... BUT DUAL ABILITY

But can the Christian love God with all the heart, soul, strength, and mind, and his neighbor as himself, with a sweet, victorious spirit in all circumstances? This we question. Some may part of the time, but not consistently. Those who do not strive for such a high level of victory are never found seeking a deeper work of grace. But is it not a fact that those who *do* seek are on their knees precisely because of their deep distress over their failure to attain the victory they have been earnestly striving for?

It is proper therefore to speak of the Christian's *failure*. It is not such a failure as to bar him from heaven should he die suddenly, for the soul who is longing for heart purity, and in the meanwhile walking the path of holy living, is already on the highway of holiness in sufficient degree to be assured of the covering Blood—but not in sufficient degree for him, while yet living, to be *satisfied*. He sees that what he experiences and practices, while genuine and wonderful, and conforming to the *ABC* of righteousness, does not measure up to the full New Testament standard. Nor does it measure up to what he *wants*.

But it is futile to discuss what an unsanctified child of God *can* or *cannot* do. Suffice it to say that in actual fact he does not possess perfect love. The thesis of this chapter is that (1) such failure is more or less *characteristic* of all first-stage Christians, that (2) the failure is due to an inherited defective moral condition, and therefore (3) the failure will persist in some measure until the defective state has been remedied. We will now examine some concrete case histories of the "Christian's failure."

Some New Testament Failures

The disciples. In the visible and personal presence of Jesus the disciples (it might be said) had a special advantage, so that failure with them was all the more shameful and puzzling. Certainly the *genuineness* of their love for the Lord cannot be seriously questioned. Neither can one challenge the vitality of their faith, in spite of their limited understanding of its implications (Matt. 16:16; John 6:6-9).

That before the death and resurrection of Jesus they were fair samples of true regeneration has been doubted by some, on the supposition that "the new birth" as such was not possible until after the atonement was completed. This is a theological issue that cannot be debated here. It cannot be denied, however, that there were certain indications of a basic change of heart prior to the Resurrection.

In the light of the biblical record, it seems logical to suppose that at least most of the disciples experienced repentance and forgiveness of sins under John's ministry.[2] It is certain that when Jesus called them they forsook all and followed Him (Matt. 4:19; 9:9; 19:27-29). Later Jesus endued them with supernatural power for service (Matt. 10:1). But when they returned full of elation, Jesus insisted that the true ground for rejoicing was not that the devils were subject to them (which would hardly have been possible had they still belonged to Satan!—cf. Acts 19:13-16), but that their names were written in heaven (Luke 10:20). Later in the Upper Room, Jesus affirms His union with them (John 15:5) and in the following prayer their alienation from the world (17:6, 9).

But with all this they failed to exhibit consistently the spirit of divine love stipulated in the great commandments. We cannot fully explain their failure by saying it was due to ignorance, misunderstanding, and inexperience. It is clear by our Lord's sharp reproofs that He at times was disappointed in them; evidently He believed He had a right to expect something better. There was a fault deep in themselves—in their spirit— which grieved the Lord.

1. This is manifest in their recurrent *hardness of heart* (Mark 6:52; 8:17). There was an inherent spiritual slowness, or lag, with a consequent tendency to unbelief. And amazingly, this tendency was not only noticeable before the Crucifixion but persisted even after the Resurrection (Luke 24:25).

2. This failure is also seen in their *spirit of rivalry and self-seeking*. They repeatedly fell short of brotherly love (Matt. 18:1; Mark 9:34; Luke 9:46). Even the hallowed and solemn Passover Feast, when Jesus instituted the Lord's Supper, was disgraced by the old strife among them "which of them should be accounted the greatest" (Luke 22:24). Apparently their love for Jesus and their sacrificial devotion to His cause were mixed

[2]Mark 1:4-5; Luke 3:2; John 1:35-37.

with generous amounts of personal ambition, as evidenced by Peter's bartering: "We have forsaken all . . . what shall we have therefore?" (Matt. 19:27) There was tin hidden in their silver, dross in their gold.

This spirit of self-seeking and rivalry also persisted after the Resurrection. Following Peter's burst of affection when he cast himself into the sea to get to Jesus first, and after Jesus had commissioned him with the words, "Feed my sheep," and even predicted his mode of martyrdom, suddenly his old jealousy flared. Glaring at John he said, "Lord, what shall this man do?" (John 21:21) How utterly unseemly in such an atmosphere! What a petty carnal spirit! Evidently his great joy that Jesus was alive—even his faith in Him as God—was not sufficient to expel from his heart this lurking selfishness. But Peter was not the last Christian to be cursed by the disease of "self-protectivitis"!

3. Then, there is the shadow of shame which passes across the pages of the Gospels as the narrative approaches the Cross. In spite of their sincere intentions and loud boasts, the disciples failed in the crisis when their Friend and Master needed them most. In the hour of peril, their bravery vanished, and with it their loyalty and fidelity. "They all forsook him, and fled." Peter with an oath denied that he ever knew Him. Plainly there was a cowardly and *traitorous element* deep in their souls with which they had not reckoned. In the sudden, unexpected turn of events it betrayed them. Looking back later on their failure they would have agreed with W. E. Sangster: "No man knows what is in him." But Jesus knew. And knowing, He prayed, "Sanctify them"—exactly the same prayer that later His chief apostle would pray for his spiritual children (I Thess. 5:23).

The failure of the disciples to love each other as themselves, thus fulfilling the second commandment, is obvious. Not quite so plain is the connection between their personal clashes and the first commandment. But the connection is there and can be stated in this way: If they had loved God with all their hearts, they would have been so preoccupied with concern for the glory of God that questions of personal advantage and power would have been forgotten.

The Corinthians. Whatever objections might be raised against citing the disciples (before Pentecost) as examples of the believer's "failure," the Corinthian Christians are certainly acceptable subjects. They were altogether in this dispensation with no overlapping overtones to confuse the issue. Their regeneration was incontestable. Paul calls them "babes in Christ" (I Cor. 3:1), and affirms that Christ was their spiritual Foundation and they "God's building" (3:6-11). He testifies further in their behalf: "And such were some of you: but ye are washed, but ye are sanctified, but ye are justified in the name of the Lord Jesus, and by the Spirit of our God" (6:11).[3] To know what these believers *had* been, one needs only to read verses 9-10. Clearly their transformation was mighty and profound.

Yet they slipped into shameful bickering and divisions, in which they "walked as men" and were a miserable discredit to the Christ whose name they bore.

1. *Old Shylock* was still in their hearts, as evidenced by their determination to defend their rights and get their "pound of flesh," even if they had to haul their brother into a pagan court to do it (6:6-8). Perfect love for either God or man would have prompted them to forego justice a thousand times rather than to bring dishonor to Christ!

---

[3]The sanctification here referred to is *initial*, not *entire;* it is that cleansing from acquired depravity which is essential if sinners are to become "as little children" (Matt. 18:3).

2. In them too, as in the pre-Pentecost disciples, we see that strangely abnormal spiritual *dullness* (I Cor. 2:6, 15; 3:1-2), with its side effects of arrested development (they were yet babes but shouldn't have been) and spiritual infantilism (still on "milk"—couldn't stand "meat," v. 2). It is easy to talk about Christians growing in grace, but in actual fact the growth of believers not wholly sanctified is very, very slight! Generally it is more a matter of going in circles, or going from one "bottle" to another. Paul said he had to "speak" to them as to babes. Newborn spiritual babes are sweet, but old ones are not. Some church members were discussing their corporate problems, when one zealous brother remarked, "What this church needs is a lot of new babes in Christ!" Whereupon an elderly mother in Israel responded: "I don't know what we would do with them; the cradles are all full now!"

3. They were like the disciples also in their *quarrelsomeness* with each other. This smallness of mind and soul, which engenders "envying, and strife, and divisions," generally accompanies arrested spiritual development. But it is also absolute proof, says Paul, of a "carnal" state (I Cor. 3:3-4). Elsewhere these sorry traits and outbreaks are listed as "works of the flesh" (Gal. 5:19-21). Their exhibition is therefore evidence of a certain remaining bondage to sin. Such a carnal state is far below the New Testament standard of life and experience. It is *sub-spiritual,* says Paul in I Corinthians 2 and 3. Yet the *spiritual* state is the Christian norm: "to be spiritually minded is life and peace" (Rom. 8:6; see also Jas. 3:13-19).

Paul affirms in I Cor. 2:6 that such spirituality was actually enjoyed by some Christians: "Howbeit we speak wisdom among them that are perfect"—by which he means the "spiritual," as is made clear in the balance of the chapter. He *can* speak the deep things of God among the spiritual, but not to most of the Corinthians. How marked is the contrast between the enlarged capacity and spiritual perception of the *spiritual* Christian and the puny appetite and infantile understanding of the carnal Christian! It is clear that in Paul's mind the distinction between normal Christian experience and subnormal carnality is sharp and unmistakable. There are obviously two classes of Christians. It is also clear that a church rent by envying and strife is not fully post-Pentecostal, or fully New Testament, no matter how loudly it may claim to be, or how many "gifts" may seem to be in evidence.

What About Christians Today?

Modernize the English, eliminate all names and place references, and the Bible descriptions of the disciples and the Corinthians could be a picture of many of today's churches. The same dullness about spiritual things, the same covetousness and worldly-mindedness, the same envying and quarreling, the same suspicion and intrigue, the same flaring resentments cripple today's Christians. They are even in evidence in the ministry. To compile case histories is too easy, too painful, and too embarrassing. Therefore let us be precise but impersonal about the chronic failure of too many Christians.

1. They fail to grow in grace in a satisfactory way. The things which defeated them five years ago still defeat them today.

2. They fail to maintain a steadfast purpose to go through with God at all costs. Sometimes the cost seems too much, and they secretly vacillate, even strongly feel the pull of the old life. At times spiritual life is at such a low ebb that they are not quite sure whether they want to go on or not. Then periodically they are warmed up, maybe at the altar in revival meeting, or at home, and take fresh hold. Soon the momentum

slows up again and the spiritual lethargy sets in. They are not stable, but "up and down."

3. They fail sometimes to conquer the deep-down covetousness in their hearts. Material values loom large in their thinking, and they find great difficulty in putting God and the church first. At times they are tempted to begrudge the time and energy which the Lord claims; they would rather spend it making more money. They are restless with desires for more and more gadgets, and finer and finer things. The appeal of sports and pleasures vies strongly on Sunday with the appeal of the house of God. Tithing is difficult for them; they resent money appeals in the church, especially sermons on the subject.

4. They often fail to keep selfish interests out of the way. Success in the eyes of man is very important to them, alarmingly so. Position and power allure strongly, even church positions which throw them into the limelight. They swagger a bit about what they know or what they own. They can't play "second fiddle" or accept rebuffs kindly.

5. They do not always keep a humble and forgiving spirit. They brood easily, and tend to smoulder for days over petty injustices. They become abnormally touchy and irritable for no real reason. They have little patience for the inconsistencies and failures of fellow Christians.

6. They fail in being deeply spiritual. They tend to neglect prayer; in fact only occasionally do they receive any real blessing in prayer. Spiritual things are not as attractive to them as they know they ought to be. The prayer meeting is often neglected for more interesting activities. Family worship may be forgotten altogether. Seldom do such persons read a devotional book, and not much of the Bible. Sometimes they sense a grave lack, and become genuinely concerned; but generally they are too busy to do anything about it, so accept the status quo.

7. Some of these carnal believers fail to witness or maintain a real concern for the unsaved. Their public testimony tends to become stale and perfunctory. Their witness at the office or factory is spotty—smudged by weak silence at times and general anxiety to be popular with the gang in spite of being a Christian.

Not all Christians, who have truly been born again, fail in all these ways, necessarily, but all tend to fail in some of them, at least part of the time (and part of the time is too much). These failures are very grave indeed. Their seriousness cannot be overdrawn. Something desperately needs to be done!

Summary

1. If the Christian's "failure" consists only in having not yet reached full maturity, it is nothing to worry about, as long as he is spiritually "on the move."

2. Neither is the failure blameworthy if it is failure to reach the standard of absolute perfection, since such failure is unavoidable.

3. But the failure in the Christian life which is serious is falling short of God's standard of divine love, toward either God or man. God requires a love which is both holy and fervent, expressed in obedience, good works, unbroken trust, and seen in spiritual-mindedness and victory.

4. It is possible for the Christian who has been born again but not filled with the Spirit to "keep going" and maintain a justified relationship with God—even, in fact, enjoy a measure of usefulness in the Lord's work. But as long as inbred sin remains, the victory will be partial, especially in the inner life, and quite unsatisfactory to a true believer.

5. His sense of need will sharpen when he sees clearly that there are not two standards, a high one for

the wholly sanctified and a low one for him; that the second work of grace does not make religion more difficult, but easier; not more complicated by the imposition of a lot of new rules, but much simpler by the unifying of the heart.

6. In a general way, the disciples before Pentecost and the Corinthian believers were typical of all unsanctified Christians, of every age, in the many ways in which their remaining sinfulness of heart revealed itself in everyday life. This outward inconsistency and inconstancy, caused by the inward double-mindedness, grieves God, misrepresents Jesus, and hinders the Church. It makes the full release of divine power upon them inadvisable and their full usefulness impossible.

QUESTIONS FOR DISCUSSION

1. What was the failure of the church at Ephesus? at Sardis (Revelation 2; 3)? Can these failures be seen today?

2. How do sinful failures on the part of Christians contribute to the feebleness of the modern Church?

3. Is there a tendency for Christians who do not profess holiness to expect less of themselves than they would if they made such a profession? If so, does this reflect on their state of justification, or merely indicate an intellectual misapprehension?

4. Is there a connection between spiritual growth *in* the Church and the growth *of* the Church in effective evangelism?

CHAPTER THREE

In Search for the Cause

Scriptures for background:

Jer. 17:9-10; Mark 7:14-23; Acts 5:1-11; Rom. 7:7—8:39; Jas. 4:1—10 (RSV)

It is always possible to pin the blame for the Christian's failure on something which happened, or on some blundering person who got in the way just at the wrong time. Too often this is exactly what the defeated Christian himself does. He rationalizes, and consequently is full of tricks. He always has an explanation for his bitterness, or sharp tongue, or his twists and turns. But the more he hides behind his alibis, the more confused becomes his spiritual life.

Sometimes even religious teachers can produce ego-salving props for the misbehaving Christian. "After all, the Corinthians had just recently been saved out of raw, barbarous paganism. You couldn't expect them to do any better!" *But Paul did.* Or, "You must take into consideration his background! He was spoiled, you know.

Give him time and he will get over his selfishness." But some have been "getting over it" for many years now, with little visible improvement.

Such leaders would be wiser to try to help under-par Christians stop looking at people and circumstances, and begin looking within. For that is what they must do in soul-wrenching honesty and humility.

SOME PLAUSIBLE ALIBIS

But even when we look "within" it is possible to come up with the wrong diagnosis. For example, the Christian's failure may be ascribed to (1) immaturity, (2) temperament, (3) physical condition.

1. Is the problem of a Christian's failing simply a matter of *newness?* If so, more practice and experience in the Christian way will remedy it. Is it ignorance only —ignorance of the Bible and Satan and the world? Then in that case intense application to study will remedy his deficiency and in so doing will sweeten his disposition.

2. Or is the problem basically a matter of natural *temperament* which time and maturity will discipline? Is *wrong training* the culprit? This often is offered as an explanation for the spitefulness and self-assertion and insubordination of the out-of-joint Christian. Or are some believers constantly full of doubts and uncertainties and arguments and objections simply because they are *superior thinkers?* If such is the cause, then to become a saint the super-intellectual either should stop thinking or find all the answers. The achievement of sainthood would thus depend on acquiring large amounts of training and knowledge.

But anyone who knows human nature and has studied Christians is painfully aware that these are not the paths to sainthood. The trained, skillful, experienced, knowledgeable, and positionally "secure" Christians can be as proud, self-seeking, unloving, and carnally cantankerous as anyone. If holiness and Christlikeness are only a matter of natural disposition, then many Christians will never be Christlike, for they were not fortunate enough to be born with the right disposition. In that case the great commandments will seem unfair to them.

3. There is yet another possible explanation for the Christian's failure: *physical condition.* The wear and tear of life, the strain on one's nervous system, the usual tensions and anxieties bring one to breakdowns, impatience, and unkindness. All men have their limit, it is often said; they can "take" only so much. When that time comes something snaps, and usually it is their religion. It may be in the form of a blowup or in the form of collapse of confidence. Weariness makes depression easy; depression makes doubt easy; doubt leads to darkness. The whole problem (seen in this light) is caused by our being so utterly human. One day a Christian may be a shining saint, with Christlikeness and love exuding from him. But this is because he *feels* good; he had a good night's rest, and his liver is in good order. The next week physical sluggishness may change his mood completely, and in his headachy, nervous jumpiness he will scream at the children.

Old-fashioned people kept praying about these changes in moods and eruptions of ugliness until God either delivered them or gave the grace for self-discipline. These days we have gotten "wise"; we take a pill. Or at least we have a physical explanation for all our reactions. But let us beware lest we surrender our souls to the behaviorists and the materialists. If this is the full explanation, then our "saintliness" is purely a psychosomatic phenomenon, and our "Christlikeness" is merely mental health. Good religion becomes more dependent upon the right doctor than upon the right creed. But in this case also the soul is epiphenomenal—we are but blobs of animated matter in a deterministic universe, and the idea of "grace" is an illusion.

But the Christian knows better than this. He knows that somewhere entangled with his upset liver, jangled nerves, and weariness and headache, is a responsible moral agent whom God expects to keep right on trusting and loving in spite of it all, and who is keenly aware of sin when he doesn't. The godless psychiatrist may advise, "Blow your top!" "It will be good for you to get it off your chest!" But the puzzled Christian does not feel that his explosion has been "good" for him or anyone else. In his heart of hearts he cannot escape the conviction that surely there is a better way.

But we must back up now to concede that our physical state and the wear and tear of life do have a lot to do with our feelings. Because of this, it is true, we do need to learn to *live*—to negotiate life as wise men and women. We need to get the proper rest, learn when to stop, learn how to relax, learn how to pray and meditate, to feed on the Scriptures, to eat sensibly, and, above all, learn to understand and discipline our moods.

But is this the total problem?

If the Christian's failure can be explained solely in terms of his haphazardness and his failure to understand himself and his moods, then of course it is obvious that the cure for his failure is simply growth in grace, with generous amounts of discipline. Efficiency, quietness, and poise, irradiated by love with all of its prismatic colors, will gradually emerge out of the learning process. All we need to do is give ourselves a little time. The hectic and lawless elements of our souls will disappear when once we get our work and time well organized and regulated. If we have been tied up inwardly with resentments and fears and bitterness, they will dissolve with improved poise and mature understanding. This, of course, is what we would call the achievement of saintliness by growth. This is entirely reasonable on the supposition that the regenerated Christian is basically sound with nothing *fundamentally* wrong with him. But this is precisely the problem.

A house occupied by the right owner and built on the right site, and *basically* sound, may need only a little paint. But if the timbers are weak and termites are boring, that is something else.

The Christian "temple" belongs to the right owner, and is built on the right site, but is it thoroughly *sound?*

What is the cause of the Christian's failure?

THE BIBLE ANSWER

Christians will prefer face-saving explanations, and to begin with often will try to solve their problems on the basis of them. So they will study, pray, throw themselves zealously into the Lord's work, and accelerate spiritual activity in general, trying to elude the wobble in the wheel. But if they take God's promises and commands seriously and if they take their failure seriously, they will sooner or later be tempted to despair. As they come to see that increased knowledge and skill have not cleansed them from their inner sinful attitudes, or cured their selfish traits, they may become disillusioned. But at this point they will begin to see that, while the *occasions* which stimulate these sinful attitudes and selfish traits may be many and varied, these occasions are not the *cause.* The cause lies farther back, deep in the self-nature. If the Christian gets wise to himself to this extent he will begin to doubt the magic efficacy of time, growth, and discipline as his sanctifiers. He may suspect a crookedness in the axle of the soul that mere acceleration will not straighten out.

At this stage he may have some measure of sympathetic understanding of Oswald Chambers, who reached the same place after four years of Christian living. He came to the desperate conclusion that if what he had "was all the Christianity there was, the thing was a fraud."[1] This is a little reminiscent of the anguished cry in Rom. 7:24: "O wretched man that I am! who shall deliver me from the body of this death?"

No, sound holiness and perfect love come as gifts of divine grace through the Holy Spirit, and not as achievements dependent on either time, growth, or purely human advantages. Yet it is obvious that sufficient grace is not experienced in conversion or the new birth. What is the impediment?

The Bible teaches that the real underlying cause of chronic failure in the Christian life is *an inherited evil bias in one's moral nature, not remedied by regeneration.*

An evil heart. Jeremiah paints a dismal picture of the human heart. He says it is "deceitful above all things, and desperately wicked: who can know it?" (17:9) Jesus does not relieve the picture at all. He says: "For from within, out of the heart of men, proceed evil thoughts, adulteries, fornications, murders, thefts, covetousness . . . pride, foolishness" (Mark 7:21-22). Yet some of these evidences of evil cropped out in both the disciples and the Corinthians. This would prove that, no matter how radically changed they were in heart, they were not entirely changed. This makes all the more significant the adjective *pure,* in Matt. 5:8 and I Tim. 1:5. It is even more significant in Acts 15:9, when the full cleansing of the heart is tied in with the baptism with the Holy Spirit. It is clear that a principle of evil still lurks in a heart which may be regenerated, yet not filled with the Holy Spirit. There is a backsliding tendency in the heart!

The carnal mind. In Rom. 8:5-7, Paul speaks of the carnal mind, by which he means, not the intellect, but the disposition, tendency, or inclination of the soul. The

[1] Quoted by Paul Rees, *Stand Up in Praise to God* (Grand Rapids: Wm. B. Eerdmans Publishing Company, 1960), p. 91.

carnal mind is the disposition to seek the fleshly pattern of living. It is that nature which is perversely responsive to sin. It is downward, earthly, and physical in its tendencies.

The unholiness of the carnal mind is seen in its essential and spontaneous antagonism to God; it "is enmity against God: for it is not subject to the law of God, neither indeed can be" (v. 7). Dr. Samuel Young speaks of this mind as "the principle that wars against the will of God." Again he defines it as "the loadstone to evil."

Quite obviously this is not a specific evil action, but the selfish bias *behind* the evil action. In this sense it is what a man *is* more than what he does. One is the root, the other the fruit.

The law of sin. Paul also calls this evil propensity "the law of sin." This discussion is in Rom. 7:7—8:4. Here, too, Paul talks about sin, not as a series of individual acts, but as a *bent to sin* which prompts the acts. This bent is not an occasional quirk, but the universal trait of the human race, and a constant moral quality in every individual of the race. This is why Paul calls it the "sin that dwelleth in me." It is not a "law" in the sense of a statute which has been passed, but a law like gravitation. This means that a man *finds* it within himself; he does not create it. It means further that its operation is uniform and predictable—always in the same direction. "For I delight in the law of God after the inward man: but I see another law in my members, warring against the law of my mind, and bringing me into captivity to the law of sin which is in my members" (7:22-23).

The law of sin is truly a "body of death," for it demands ultimate and final separation from God. The same thing is said of the carnal mind, which is obviously the law of sin under a different name: "To be carnally minded is death." Unless therefore there is a way to be rid of the carnal mind, the infected believer still has the sentence of death *within*, even though personal sins have been pardoned. Truly the soul needs a *double* cure —not only pardon, but purity.

This then is the substratum of sinfulness in human nature by which all men are sinners. Paul explains it this way: "But I am carnal, sold under sin" (7:14). Apart from his own volition, he was already delivered to the power of sin. Who sold him? Adam. With all other descendants of Adam, Paul shared a common bondage. The sin nature, he makes clear, was in him from birth. It did not begin in him when he committed his first sin; it was prior to it as its prompter (7:9-11).

We are reaching now the crux of the matter, and the answer to the problem of the Christian's failure. For while justification by faith deals with a man's personal guilt (those sins which he has willingly committed) and purges him from the accumulated depravity resulting from those sins, it does not cleanse his nature from the moral twist he *inherited.* Conversion makes a man become again as a "little child" (Matt. 18:3) in his simplicity of heart and cleanness before God; but it does not take him *beyond the state* of the child, which is a carnal state.

Let us put it yet another way. Regeneration imparts a new nature, inclined toward spiritual things, without totally removing the old nature. Hence it is possible for the Bible to speak of the "double minded" (Jas. 1:8; 4:8).[2] This can, of course, be interpreted as the vacillation of one who wavers because he can't quite make up his mind; and in this sense the Christian finds himself fluctuating between two opinions. But the meaning is

[2]The Greek here is not the same as in Rom. 8:5-7. It is literally "two-souled." A. T. Robertson translates it: "double-souled, double-minded, Bunyan's 'Mr. Facing-both-ways'" (*Word Pictures in the New Testament* [New York: Harper and Brothers Publishers, 1933]), VI, 15.

deeper than this. He is swinging between two *dispositions,* so that there is an inward conflict. Sometimes the carnal mind seems stronger, and at other times the new mind is stronger. But meanwhile he cannot do the things that he would.

Two patterns of living, two sets of values, as the twins struggling within Rebecca, are contesting within the Christian for absolute loyalty and complete mastery. It was this dual state which made the disciples such inconsistent and unpredictable followers of Jesus. This is why Jesus could acknowledge them as true disciples, yet pronounce them "evil" (Luke 11:13). This also explains why Paul could call the Corinthians "yet carnal." Both the disciples and the Corinthians were spiritually alive but they were not yet entirely holy in heart. This lurking carnal nature imparted an element of evil to their character, in spite of their good intentions and their love for Jesus. This inner disease "broke out" (like measles) in their "envying, and strife, and divisions."[3]

[3] In view of this, the age-old debate about Romans 7 (does it describe the carnal Christian or the awakened Jew under the law?) is a bit pointless. The chapter applies to whoever experiences the spiritual struggle described therein. And the Christian who has made an honest attempt to keep the carnal mind under, only to repeatedly fail, and who has finally seen the "groundwork of his heart" (John Wesley), will not hesitate to cry, "The picture is mine!" Of course he has a measure of victory over sin, just as did the disciples and the Corinthians, and in fact, as Paul did even before his conversion. But he will also be aware of a measure of bondage; and the more he craves holiness, the more anguished will be his cry, "O wretched man that I am!"

The only way Romans 7 can be restricted in its application to the unregenerate is to say that "indwelling sin," as an inherited principle of evil, is effectively dealt with in regeneration, so that the Christian no longer has a problem with it. If it is present it will become a problem—we can be sure of that—for it is "not subject to the law of God." But to assume that regeneration delivers from this bias to evil is to suppose an experience which neither the disciples (before Pentecost) nor the Corinthians enjoyed, and which never has been taught by any of the major

The Rebel Within

There is an interesting construction in the Greek of Paul's testimony to the Galatians: "I have been crucified with Christ: it is no longer I who live, but Christ who

orthodox creeds of Christendom. On the contrary, they have agreed that man does come into the world with a sinful bias, that it does remain in the believer's heart, and that it does, though suppressed, become the Christian's supreme problem in the new life. And *this* is the real explanation for the Christian's *failure*.

Another technical but important problem has been whether or not Paul intended to teach that indwelling sin was an entity, or *real being*. That it is not a physical entity, as a rotten tooth, is surely obvious. Therefore when thinking of its eradication we must avoid the picture of an automobile accessory, such as a battery, which can be taken out, then replaced. Neither can it be said to be a metaphysical entity, strictly speaking, unless it is actually a form of demon possession, or psychic presence, as William Sanday seems to suggest. Even so, it is not a "thing in itself" which can exist apart from moral agents. *However*, we dare not tone down Paul's strong teaching here on the nature of this indwelling sin as a dynamic moral power in the soul which is sub-volitional. Those who would explain away any positive concept of original sin have this chapter squarely in their path. Toward a helpful solution might be two propositions:

a. It is essentially a deprivation, or lack, of the Holy Spirit. Richard Watson taught that man became depraved as a result of being deprived of the Holy Spirit. But while essentially negative, it is also positive, inasmuch as human personality is inherently dynamic; this being so, a person without God will be a dynamic *evil* person. Cold is nothing but the absence of heat; nevertheless a "cold wave" is a dynamic force, as anyone who has suffered its freezing power knows.

b. It can also be thought of as a dislocation, or disorganization, of instincts and faculties of the being, *around self rather than God.* Adam's choice of self rather than God resulted in an endemic self-orientation which thereafter prevailed in the race. This, of course, is the positive depravity which stemmed racially from Adam's deprivation.

Put these two ideas together and we see that man is cursed with a BIG "I" which will never be trimmed to size until completely recaptured, repossessed, and recontrolled by the Holy Spirit.

lives in me; and the life I now live in the flesh I live by faith in the Son of God" (2:20, RSV). Notice the many first-person pronouns used. But in the Greek the word for *I* (*ego*) is used only once—and that is the "I" which is slain on the Cross! Every other "I" is hidden in a verb, completely out of sight! Phillips brings out this remarkable distinction this way: "And my present life is not that of the old 'I,' but the living Christ within me."

Sometimes, it is true, we use the term "ego" as a synonym for the self, and that, as a metaphysical entity, is indestructible. Without the ego in this sense we would be nonexistent as persons. But Paul in this verse *seems* to be giving the word a spiritual connotation; he associates it with an evil, past self, which has been put away. He is still a person—still a metaphysical self—so can still refer to himself. But the *ego,* as constituting an independent self-centeredness, a hard core of self-idolatry, in other words, the "BIG I," is gone. Immediately we think of some rather uncomplimentary modern variations: *egoism,* which the dictionary defines as excessive self-interest; and *egotism,* which we quickly recognize as a synonym for conceit.

This "BIG I" is seen to be nothing other than the "law of sin," the "carnal mind," and the "evil heart of unbelief," with the mask off. It is the disposition to relate everything to self and its interests, to a selfish and rebellious degree. The very essence of this indwelling sin therefore is a fundamental bent toward self-authority or self-sovereignty. John calls it "lawlessness" (I John 3:4, RSV). Paul (as we have noted before) says it is not "subject to the law of God, neither indeed can be" (Rom. 8:7). For in its very nature it is rebellion. Paul Updike says: "The spirit of independency is of the essence of carnality." Its sinfulness lies in the fact that whether intended or not, or fully realized or not, this independency is toward God as well as toward men. A spirit of independency toward men might in some circumstances be necessary, but a resistance to God's yoke is sinful.

Pride and unbelief are inseparable aspects of this inner core of self-willfulness and self-love. Pride exalts self as the supreme value, while unbelief exalts self as the supreme authority. Men do not believe God because they would rather believe themselves.

Let us see how this self-exaltation lines up with Rom. 12:1-2. William L. Bradley says: "The Cross is not only an event in history (though certainly it is not less than this), but it is repeated in climactic fashion in every human situation when men come face to face with the ultimate problem of Self." This, he goes on to say, arouses a "deadly inner conflict," which man naturally tries to evade by retreating to the safety of abstract truth and academic discussions. "It is not easy," he says, "to be faced with questions of ultimate concern when they confront us with the fact of an inevitable death which will wrench us from the treasures we have industriously collected for ourselves." The real struggle is in giving up what Oswald Chambers calls "our right to ourselves." Bradley expresses it vividly: "What assurance have we that there will be anything left of us if we sacrifice every shred of selfhood, of self-respect, of the 'I' which at least we can claim as our very own? No one can take our last bit of pride from us, and here is Christ demanding that we give it up to God right now." What is the spontaneous reaction of the carnal self to this radical demand? "Naturally we strike back at Him," is the way Bradley puts it. "Quite normally we reject Him at this point."[4]

This irrational struggle of the Christian who has once said, "Yes," with a remaining inward "No" can be

[4]Excerpts from "The Authority of Jesus Christ," by William L. Bradley (professor of the philosophy of religion and chairman of the faculty of Hartford Theological Seminary), *Hartford Review*, 3rd quarter, 1961. Quoted by permission.

seen in the concrete reactions of some representative persons. Fred Dalzell, a converted Communist, testifies in the *Flame* that after he was saved he became aware of his spiritual lack, and of an increasing hunger for the fullness of the Holy Spirit. In a service one day, he says, "the challenge was made to seek full salvation; but my heart remained stubborn..."

David Ramirez, a Harvard Ph.D. who became the founder of Nazarene missions in his native Nicaragua, heard H. V. Miller preach on holiness in Chicago. Though he had been converted as a youth, and had recently been reclaimed after many years of wandering, this was his first exposure to the doctrine of entire sanctification. His trained mind (a doctorate both in philosophy and psychology) instantly grasped the radical implications of what Dr. Miller was saying. He reacted violently. On the way home he protested to his friend that Dr. Miller was wrong; that no one should so completely surrender himself, not even to God! A week of Bible study attempting to disprove the preacher resulted in intense conviction instead, and the next Sunday found him at the public altar making the very absolute surrender which his carnal heart had so violently protested.[5]

This state in which there are both a "yes" and a "no" struggling for final supremacy in the heart will not be a permanent state. There will be a victor. If the "no" is final victor, then Christ and the Christian are defeated. For, to quote again from William L. Bradley: "In asserting the autonomy of our wills we destroy the possibility of our spiritual freedom. We reject—we disclaim—what we know to be our true destiny." Therefore no inquiry could be more crucial than this inquiry into the nature of the believer's failure—or rather the nature

[5]See *To Live Is Christ,* by Helen Temple (Kansas City: Beacon Hill Press, 1961). Ruth Paxson tells of a similar experience in her own Christian life in *Rivers of Living Water.*

of its *cause*. Only then can we inquire concerning a cure. "The answer to the problem of true life," concludes Bradley, "thus lies at the center of the self and its ultimate loyalty."

SUMMARY

1. If a better experience is going to be found, carnal believers must refuse to blame their spiritual failures on secondary factors, such as temperament, ignorance, or physical health.

2. That these factors are important is not denied; in fact their subtle way of influencing our conduct will be discussed in a later chapter. But they are secondary to the deeper problem.

3. The primary cause is indwelling sin, an inherited evil bias toward self-willfulness, or tendency toward excessive self-love. This remains after regeneration in its original inherited degree. Though its power is broken, to the extent that it no longer rules completely, its power is not totally destroyed.

QUESTIONS FOR DISCUSSION

1. Does it generally take long for a soundly converted new Christian to discover there is yet something deeply wrong in his heart?

2. Is this discovery made by Christians in non-holiness groups, or only where holiness is preached? Can any examples be cited?

3. Do the noticeable traits of the carnal mind vary in different people? Often a "bad temper" is emphasized, as if this were the main trait. What others can you name?

4. If not yet sanctified, what do you see in yourself? If God has brought you into perfect rest of soul, what grieved you (and Him) before you obtained deliverance?

CHAPTER FOUR

The Divine Provision

Scriptures for background:

Mal. 3:1-4; John 1:1-34; Acts 2:14-39; Heb. 10:14-25

Having seen the New Testament standard of Christian life and experience, and having been made aware that the Christian has still a spiritual lameness, we must now ask very earnestly whether God has provided a cure for the lameness. We believe He has.

"For the law was given by Moses, but grace and truth came by Jesus Christ" (John 1:17). There was plenty of high moral standard in Moses but *little power*. Sufficient ability and satisfactory fulfillment are made possible by Jesus. Every Christian has tasted the goodness of this grace in the new birth. He needs only to see that Jesus has all-sufficient power for every believer to go all the way to the depths of his need. There is in the atonement not only a provision for one's personal guilt and defilement, for which he is responsible, but provision for the inherited bent to sinning with which he still struggles.

Why a "New" Testament?

Pick up your Bible and take a fresh look at it. Let it fall open between Malachi and Matthew. On the left is the *Old Testament;* on the right is the *New Testa-*

ment. Since "testament" means *covenant,* we naturally are intrigued by the adjective "old." Why was the first covenant supplanted by a new one? In the old covenant was the standard of love. (See Deut. 6:5; Lev. 19:18.) That did not need replacing. The new covenant builds squarely on it. Not only so, but man's inability to meet the standard fully was repeatedly acknowledged and the problem diagnosed: "The heart is deceitful above all things, and desperately wicked: who can know it?" (Jer. 17:9)

Furthermore, man was expected to *attempt* the standard, and could approximate it, at least outwardly. Paul came quite close as a Pharisee. "Touching the righteousness which is in the law, blameless" (Phil. 3:6), he testifies. So also did Moses and Joshua, to say nothing of Noah, Job, Abraham, and others who were righteous even before the law was formally given at Sinai. But these towering saints represent rare exceptions. Satisfactory fulfillment did not characterize the old-covenant worshippers.[1]

---

[1] It is believed by some that these Old Testament saints experienced by faith the full blessing of heart holiness, and thus experienced the Pentecost blessing in pre-Pentecostal times. But this does not represent the normal experience of devout Israelites; it seemed to be an exceptional attainment of a very few. But in the dispensation of the Holy Spirit the situation is reversed; the fullness of the blessing is intended as the norm for the many. Nothing less than this can be the meaning of Joel: "I will pour out my spirit upon all flesh . . ." (Joel 2:28-29; Acts 2:16-18). All worshippers, even the sons and daughters, "servants" and "handmaidens," young men and old men, may now have equal access to the sanctifying fullness of the Spirit, and enjoy as much intimacy with God as the special saints of the Old Testament. The ministry of the Spirit before Christ was deep but necessarily limited. The full outpouring on "all flesh" was not possible before the Cross and the Resurrection. But this outpouring meant a removing of the limitations upon the Spirit's personal redemptive ministry. It thus meant a diffusion of His sanctifying power to all men, and a completely impartial access by all believers.

But it is important to see that if an honest attempt was all that mattered, and an *approximation* would satisfy God, a *new covenant* would in that case not be needed. But God was not satisfied with an approximation. Therefore He provided something better in Christ. This was fulfillment at the very point of failure, by rectifying the defect in man's nature.

That this inner soundness was the paramount purpose of a new covenant, rather than pardon alone, is incontestably affirmed in *both* Testaments. Describing the new covenant God plans for His people, Jeremiah pinpoints it: "I will put my law in their inward parts, and write it in their hearts" (Jer. 31:33). Ezekiel says the same thing: "And I will put my spirit within you, and cause you to walk in my statutes" (36:27). This promise is associated with an indispensable renovation of nature, consisting of the impartation of a "new heart" and the complete removal of "the stony heart" (v. 26). Malachi specifically points to the Messiah as the One by whom these promises will be fulfilled (Mal. 3:1-3).

The New Testament states clearly that these promises (and many others like them) find their fulfillment in Christ, and that such fulfillment constitutes the very essence of the new covenant which God promised (Luke 1:73-75; Acts 2:16 f.; Heb. 8:10; 10:16; I Tim. 1:5 f.).

There was provision under Moses for the pardon of man's personal sins, but no provision for the correction of his inherited sinfulness. But in the New Testament this lack is not only supplied; it is the *heart* of God's total provision in Christ. This is a very startling and basic truth. It means that those Christian teachers who see no immediate cure for the believer's lameness, and who are content with only an attempt and an approximation of perfect love as the best that can be expected in this life, are still living and thinking in the Old Testament. They may ardently accept and love Jesus, but they have reduced Him to an Old Testament Saviour.

They have missed utterly the full power and glory of His grace. Jesus did not suffer and die to make a mere approximation acceptable, but to make true holiness possible. And this was not His secondary but His primary mission. Let us get into the New Testament!

ERADICATION VERSUS SUPPRESSION OR COUNTERACTION

There are three technical terms used by Bible teachers which represent different theories concerning God's method of dealing with the sinful heart. These three terms are suppression, counteraction, and eradication.

According to the *suppression* theory, God's grace will help us restrain our evil propensities, and achieve a measure of victory, though it will never be complete or entirely satisfactory. This is the picture of a man sitting on a lid that is about to blow off because of seething steam within.

According to the *counteraction* theory the power of the carnal mind is nicely balanced by the power of the indwelling Holy Spirit, so that the activity of the carnal mind is neutralized. This is the picture of a teeter-totter with the man on one end perfectly balanced by a man of equal weight on the other. By and large this is the view of the Keswick Conventions in England, Australia, and elsewhere.

Those however who believe in *eradication* maintain that man's nature must be thoroughly corrected by the elimination of the inner sinfulness itself.

Suppression. Confusion arises by the fact that all three views contain elements of truth when properly interpreted. Take first the idea of suppression. Paul said, "But I keep under my body, and bring it into subjection" (I Cor. 9:27). Even a holy man must control and restrain his natural appetites. Right here is one of the major fallacies of both the suppressionist and the counteractionist: the assumption that sinfulness is so inseparably and unalterably a part of our earthly nature that only death can deliver us. This is a very serious error. Paul was not necessarily sinful simply because he needed to keep his body under. Adam and Eve were holy, yet needed to keep their bodies under and failed to do so. The Lord Jesus suppressed His natural appetite in the wilderness when Satan suggested that the stones be turned into bread. His hunger was not sinful, but He rejected a method of satisfaction suggested by Satan, rather than one provided by God. In this sense He was doing exactly what Paul said he did, "I keep my body under," by which he meant, "I keep the natural man subservient to the perfect will of God." This is what holy men always must do, but they are not necessarily thereby saying that they are "keeping under" a *sinful* nature.

A young woman, brought up in the suppressionist school of thought, argued with the writer on this doctrinal point, and finally said, "If all sin is removed from the heart, what is there left?" She seemed to feel that man was *sin* "by definition," and if sin were removed man would be extinguished. This is a totally false concept of both human nature and sin. A simple illustration will help us to see this more clearly. When we taste ocean water we taste saltiness. We never escape this saltiness in the ocean whether we taste the Pacific or the Atlantic, whether we sample it on the shore or out in the depths, whether we taste it in the storm or in the calm; it is universally and always salty. So if a person had never known anything but ocean water, he would be inclined to define water as a salty liquid. But this is not so. What is left after the salt has been removed? Why, water! It is now for the first time in a state of normalcy, palatable and fresh as water in its pure state is. So men who have been purified from sin are not unnatural, but natural. They are not less human, but more naturally human, for the inhuman and unnatural propensities of the carnal mind have distorted and perverted true human nature. Now having been cleansed, true human nature is released, and can develop properly.

Counteraction. There is likewise an element of truth in the theory of counteraction. Evan H. Hopkins, one of the early leaders of the Keswick movement, used the illustration of a piece of lead floating on the water by means of a lifebelt. Its tendency to sink is counteracted by the lifebelt. In similar fashion our tendency to sin is counteracted by the indwelling Holy Spirit.[2] We fully admit that apart from the indwelling presence of the Holy Spirit man is morally *leaden.* But that was just as true before the fall of Adam as after, of *holy* human nature as well as unholy. It is true of all created moral beings. Without hesitation we concede that when the Holy Spirit is withdrawn or repelled man's nature immediately sinks into depravity. If this is what we mean by the "tendency" to sin, then of course the tendency to sin is universal and ineradicable. However at this point sound holiness writers and teachers have never had any quarrel. It was William Booth who admonished, "Watch the fire on the altar of your soul; the tendency of fire is to go out!" Certainly we must maintain constantly the fullness of the Holy Spirit or our purified souls will again become defiled. In this sense "counteraction" is an acceptable theory, for man certainly has no holiness that is self-originating or self-perpetuating.[3]

Eradication. To talk about counteracting a tendency to fall apart from the presence and power of God is altogether different from the supposition that the Spirit must counteract an active, dynamic disposition toward sinful self-will which continues in the heart. We are

[2]*The Law of Liberty in the Spiritual Life* (London: Marshall, Morgan & Scott, Ltd., n.d.), p. 111.

[3]It would be a mistake, however, to assume that the difference between the Keswick and Wesleyan views is only in terminology, or only at this point.

here confusing things which radically differ. The Bible concept of sinfulness is not this passive "tendency," for if so we must say that Adam and Eve were sinful.

A better analogy of the true situation is that of the darkness in a room which is dispelled by the incoming of light. The inner spiritual lightness of the soul is totally dependent upon the outside source of light getting in and abiding, just as is true with a room in the house. Moreover, the coming of the light has not "eradicated" the tendency of the room to be dark if cut off from its source of light. But though this "tendency" is not eradicated, *the darkness is.* A room can be partially dark and partially light, but it cannot be wholly light and at the same time be in any degree dark. And it is *darkness,* not *tendency,* which is the likeness of sin. Any degree of sin in the heart is a measure of darkness. Now read I John 1:5-7: "And this is the message that we have heard from Him and announce to you, that God is light, and in Him there is no darkness at all. If we say that we have fellowship with Him and yet walk in the darkness, we lie and do not practice the truth; but if we walk in the light as He himself is in the light, we have fellowship with one another, and the blood of Jesus Christ His Son cleanses us from all sin" (NASB).

Since darkness symbolizes sin, we can say that if "all" sin is cleansed there is no darkness "at all." Any measure of sin is a measure of darkness, which impairs our fellowship with Him—and this measure of sin is *not* cleansed by the Blood. Now turn it around: Sin that is cleansed is nonexistent. Where the light of holiness is complete, there is no darkness of sin at all. It is not counteracted, for it simply is not there. The "tendency" to again become dark should the soul reject the "light" remains; but while he is walking in the light, the darkness itself is eradicated. If one prefers, the word "dispelled" could be used, but the meaning is the same.

The conclusion of the matter therefore is that our *human nature* is to be "suppressed" in the sense of being disciplined and restrained; our dependence upon God is to be constantly remembered and our holiness sustained by the indwelling and honored presence of the Holy Spirit. But the sinful disposition itself which prompts coveting, envying, hatred, and murder is to be purged from the nature.

THE REMEDIAL TERMS IN THE BIBLE

The three terms which we have just been examining represent three doctrinal approaches to the problem of indwelling sin in the believer. The teachers who hold these views are not those who would advocate a low standard of Christian living, but they are devout men who are seeking to find the way of victorious living. They represent three theories concerning God's method of dealing with the sin nature and of helping the believer achieve this victory. Our position is unequivocally on the side of eradication as being God's method. It has certain advantages. One is that in our view it is more in harmony with both a sound doctrine of man and a sound doctrine of sin. A second advantage is that the preaching and teaching of this position seem to be more effective in helping people actually find a satisfactory experience of holiness.

But it is the third advantage which is really decisive for all Bible-believing Christians: The Bible teaches the eradication of inbred sin. Perhaps the most significant support for this assertion is found in the *remedial terms used in relation to the believer and his sin*. These terms do not suggest either suppression or counteraction, but eradication. This is true in the Old Testament promises, such as the promise to "take away the stony heart out of your flesh" (Ezek. 36:26). But let us turn now to the major terms found in the New Testament expressing God's activity in meeting the need of man's sinful nature.

Purify. The various forms of the Greek word *katharidzo* may mean (1) *ceremonial cleanness or cleansing,* as with Mary, the mother of Jesus, who was considered by Jewish law unclean for forty days after the birth of her Firstborn (Luke 2:22; cf. Mark 1:44; Luke 5:14; John 2:6); or (2) *moral innocence,* i.e., freedom from guilt, such as was the condition of the disciples in the Upper Room whom Jesus pronounced "clean through the word" (John 15:3); or the situation of Paul, who testified, "I am pure from the blood of all men" (Acts 20:26). But the most important meaning is (3) *the purging of the heart from sin.* While the disciples were purged before Pentecost in the second sense, they were purged at Pentecost in this deeper sense. This is the clear testimony of Peter in Acts 15:9, when specifying exactly what happened to both the household of Cornelius and the original Pentecost recipients. This is a divine purifying, not a self-purification. It is furthermore associated with the baptism with the Holy Spirit, not their conversion. And it is a purifying of the *heart,* which is where sin is.

The full force of this word can perhaps best be seen by pointing out that it is almost invariably the word used in reference to the healing of lepers. For instance, the ten lepers were told to appear before the priest, and we read that "as they went, they were cleansed" (Luke 17:14; also see Matt. 8:3; 10:8; 11:5; *et al.*). Was this only a physical bathing, or perhaps a mere ceremonial cleansing? On the contrary, nothing is clearer than that these lepers were *healed,* thoroughly and gloriously made sound and whole!

Whether their healing included the restoration of lost members, such as a finger or nose which had wasted away due to the ravages of the disease, we do not know. It may be that they went through life carrying with them the marks and the scars of their previous horror. But the important thing is that now they were no longer leprous. They no longer had to cry, "Unclean! Unclean!" wherever they went. The disease was not only arrested, it was eliminated. They were well. Just as leprosy is a perfect type of indwelling sin, so *katharidzo* is a perfect designation for God's method of treatment.

I once visited in the home of a man who had made quite a few changes in his house. As I admired the altered doorframes and the fresh paint job, he made this comment, "A good carpenter, you know, is known, not by what he can do, but by what he can cover up!" I was quite impressed until I visited again in the home six months later. The old stains on the wall were coming through; the rotten timbers in the doorframes had developed new cracks. I concluded that a cover-up job is poor renovation after all. Is Christ in the business of doing a cover-up job only? Does the blood of Jesus whitewash without washing white? Does the blood of Jesus cover our sin without altering the nature underneath, without replacing the rotten timbers and taking away the deep stains? No, we must reiterate that the word *purify* means to remove impurities. This is the natural sense of the word and also the scriptural sense of the word.

When Peter affirmed the disciples' purification on the Day of Pentecost he did not mean that their *minds* were purified from error, for much instruction was still needed. Nor did he mean that their *lives* were purified totally from mistaken conduct, for mistakes were still made. What he did say was that their *hearts* were purified, by which is meant their inner nature was healed and corrected.

It must be emphasized once again that the heart is where sin is. To be healed at the heart means to be cleansed of sin. It is the heart that is double-minded; therefore to be purified in heart is to be cleansed of double-mindedness. It is the heart that is proud; therefore to be purified in heart is to be cleansed of pride.

It is the heart that "is deceitful above all things, and desperately wicked"; therefore to be purified in heart is to be cleansed of deceitfulness and wickedness. A heart that has been purified is no longer double-minded, no longer proud, no longer deceitful and wicked, but is sound and whole and clean in the sight of God.

Circumcise. This term is profoundly significant both in the Old Testament and in the New Testament. Though it refers to a Hebrew rite given to Abraham by God, it suggests, in its spiritual significance, a correction of man's nature. This is made perfectly clear in Deut. 30:6, where God promises to circumcise His people in heart that they might love Him perfectly. We have already learned that the standard is perfect love. We have also seen that the impediment to the fulfillment of this standard is inbred sin. This is an abnormal condition of the heart. It is thus clear that even in the Old Testament God promises to remove this excess self-nature in order that we may be able to fulfill acceptably the great commandment. As we have already discovered, inbred sin is the sin of egoism, which the dictionary defines as "excessive self-interest." Spiritual circumcision, that which is made without hands as suggested by Col. 2:11, is the excision of this excessive self-interest, so that self is dethroned, and God is perfectly enthroned. This word no more suggests suppression or counteraction as God's method of dealing with the sin principle than does the word "purify."

Free from. A sweeping affirmation is given to us in Rom. 8:2: "For the law of the Spirit of life in Christ Jesus hath made me free from the law of sin and death." This "law of sin and death" is the very principle of indwelling sin which Paul has been describing in the previous chapter, and which we have already seen to be the cause of the Christian's failure. But God plans in Christ by the power of the Spirit to emancipate us from this inward proclivity which has been the cause of our defeat. The rest of the passage is thrillingly specific: "For what the law could not do, in that it was weak through the flesh, God sending his own Son in the likeness of sinful flesh, and for sin, condemned sin in the flesh: that the righteousness of the law might be fulfilled in us, who walk not after the flesh, but after the Spirit" (Rom. 8:3-4). Here is not an approximated righteousness but a fulfilled righteousness. This is the purpose of the atonement and the genius of divine grace in Christ. Sin in the flesh may be condemned in the sense that it may be destroyed. The word "condemned" means far more than disapprove, for Christ did not need to die to disapprove sin. It means that now at last a remedy is found for the sin principle in human nature.

Sanctify. This word can be interpreted very broadly, and made to mean not only the Christianizing of man's nature by cleansing from sin, but its development in grace of personality and strength of character. Understood in this broad sense it would include *initial* sanctification (which is experienced in regeneration), *entire* sanctification (which is experienced in a second work of grace), and *progressive* sanctification. But to avoid confusion probably we should restrict it to *being made holy* in the first and second works of grace. Basically it means "to make holy" and is so translated by Phillips. To make *holy* is to *present wholly to God,* and also to make *free from sin.* It thus has at times a sense of *consecration,* and at other times the sense of *purification.* In still other cases both ideas are implied in its use. When the Lord Jesus said, "And for their sakes I sanctify myself," He was saying, "For their sakes I consecrate myself to the task of the Cross" (John 17:19). But when He was praying for His disciples that God might sanctify *them* (17:17), He was praying not only for their consecration, but *something more.* He was praying that God through the Holy Ghost might do in them whatever needed to be done to make them holy, victorious, and useful servants in the Kingdom. This was the same burden of our Lord's chief apostle in his prayer for his Thessalonian converts, "And the very God of peace sanctify you wholly" (I Thess. 5:23). That sanctification is central and basic to God's redemptive program is obvious from such passages as II Thess. 2:15; I Thess. 4:3-8; Eph. 1:4; 3:14-21; I Pet. 1:2.

Clearly the remedial terms used in the New Testament suggest total renovation and correction. Holiness is not only imputed but must be imparted. We must say again that Jesus did not die to make partial holiness acceptable, but to make true holiness possible.

SANCTIFIED—HOW PERFECTLY?

Convincing modifiers. We can test the doctrine still further. Not only do the *remedial* terms suggest correction, but the *modifying* terms used indicate thoroughness in this connection. For instance, the word "all" is sweeping and comprehensive as used in I John 1:7-9. "All sin" means *all sin.* Likewise the word "uttermost" as used in Heb. 7:25 means that Christ is able to save those that come unto God by Him, wholly and completely.[4]

The modifying term "wholly" in I Thess. 5:23 is very significant also, for it is a compound Greek word meaning not only in every part but through and through every part. God wants no part of us unsanctified. He

[4]The translation of "uttermost" as "for all time" by the Revised Standard Version is not justified by either the Greek or the context. In the thinking of the writer of this Epistle the perpetual intercession of an ever-living Saviour is not so much seen as a surety for our *permanent* salvation (though this is implied, of course) as an assurance of a *permeating* salvation—an adequate deliverance from sin here and now. A. T. Robertson admits that the temporal idea is possible, "but," he says, "the common meaning is completely, utterly" (*Word Pictures,* V, 387). Cf. Luke 13:11, where the same Greek idiom, with the negative particle *ma,* is translated "in no wise," meaning that the afflicted woman was *utterly and completely* unable to stand up straight.

wants that there shall be no element of sinfulness lurking anywhere. The terms "spirit and soul and body," whatever else they may signify, certainly indicate the total man. The question has been asked: "Does entire sanctification include the subconscious?" The answer is already given in Paul's prayer. If the subconscious is part of the total man, then the subconscious too is to be sanctified. This does not mean of course that everything abnormal in the subconscious is instantly eliminated, for the term "abnormal" is much broader than the term "sin." Once again we must avoid confusing human nature with carnal nature, and refrain from confusing the sin principle with the scars and the marks of sin. *Love* must be in the subconscious as well as in the conscious. Hatred must be cleansed from the subconscious as well as the conscious; yet there may be peculiarities and even complexes in the subconscious which hinder the perfect outward expression of love, but which in themselves are not sinful.

Scriptural perfection. Then there is the word *perfect*, which puzzles so many people. Some would like to discard it entirely from our religious vocabulary. But what then would we do with the frequent usage of the term in the New Testament in *direct reference* to God's will and provision for man? It is thus used at least thirty-two times. Jesus was not trifling when He said, "Be ye therefore perfect, even as your Father which is in heaven is perfect" (Matt. 5:48). And Epaphras was not being impractical, idealistic, or fanatical when he prayed for the Colossians that they might "stand perfect and complete in all the will of God" (Col. 4:12). Nor was John mocking us when in the Spirit he affirmed the possibility of our love being made perfect, with that degree of perfection which casts out the fear that hath torment, and gives us calmness and assurance as we contemplate the Judgment (I John 4:17-18).

Some people, strangely enough, are more afraid of Christian perfection than they are of sinful imperfection, but they must change their attitude if they are to be acceptable to God either in heart or in theology. At the same time, however, we who use the term must be clear in our thinking that we are not professing perfection of judgment or even of conduct, for we recognize many imperfections even in the midst of Christian perfection. We must recognize that perfect motive and perfect affection toward God and toward men, with the absence of all evil tempers and ulterior motives, is that measure of purity, or that attainment in divine grace, which is God's expectation and our privilege in this life. But this is a perfection consistent with a thousand imperfections in knowledge and judgment.[5] And while the Apostle Paul disclaimed the perfection of glorification (Phil. 3:12), he unhesitatingly identified himself with the "perfect" in verse 15, indicating that there is a kind of perfection possible in this life and a kind which is impossible. That kind which is possible (and expected) we call Christian perfection.

No concept of perfection is meaningful, in any realm, except as the performance or achievement can be gauged by that known standard to which it is related. Perfection in a timepiece is related to *keeping time,* not winning a prize for artistic design. So perfection in Christians is related to the required and clearly specified

[5]In his *Plain Account of Christian Perfection,* John Wesley said: "Now, mistakes, and whatever infirmities necessarily flow from the corruptible state of the body, are noway contrary to love; nor therefore, in the Scripture sense, sin . . . I believe there is no such perfection in this life as excludes these involuntary transgressions which I apprehend to be naturally consequent on the ignorance and mistakes inseparable from mortality. . . . I believe, a person filled with the love of God is still liable to these involuntary transgressions. . . . Such transgressions you may call sins, if you please: I do not, for the reasons above-mentioned" (*Works,* XI, 396).

standard of love. It is not related to some unauthorized standard erected by some critical cynic who growls: "I never saw anyone who measured up to my ideal of a perfect Christian!" So what? The fact does not discredit either the possibility or the possession of *Christian* perfection, which is being "holy and without blame before him in love" (Eph. 1:4). Note that it says "before *him*," the One who sees the secret intent of the heart, and never misinterprets motives on the basis of appearances. Absolute perfection belongs to God only. Adamic perfection belonged to Adam only. Angelic perfection belongs to angels only. Heavenly perfection belongs to glorified saints only. But Christian perfection may and must belong to flesh-and-blood Christians, right here on earth, with all their limitations and shortcomings.

Sometimes, also, perfection is defined as *finality,* the absolute limit of possible development. When this is done it is naturally impossible to see how *perfection* can be reconciled with continued need for growth in grace. But this is a confusion of dynamic perfection, which belongs to *life,* with *static* perfection, which belongs to *things.* It is true that the term "perfect" in the Bible sometimes means "mature," but never *absolute* maturity, as if further development were now impossible. Even Paul said he was "reaching forth unto those things which are before"—yet it was in this very connection that he professed perfection (Phil. 3:13-15)!

The difference between this dynamic perfection and static perfection can be illustrated by a simple story. Three men, it is said, quarreled over a horse, a cow, and a wagon. When finally they were haled before the judge, the first was asked, "How long have you owned this horse?" and the answer was, "Your Honor, since it was a little colt." The second was asked, "How long have you owned this cow?" and the answer was, "Your Honor, since it was a little calf." The third one was asked, "How long have you owned this wagon?" and the reply was,

"Since it was a little wheelbarrow." The answers of the first two do not surprise us, but that of the third does. This is true in spite of the fact that the calf and the colt as well as the wheelbarrow might have been taken to the county fair and pronounced perfect by the judges. But no matter how perfect is a colt, we expect it to grow; no matter how perfect is a calf, we expect it to grow; in fact we expect it to grow *because* it is perfect. Its very perfection as a living creature demands growth as part of the fulfillment of its own nature. But we do not expect the wheelbarrow to grow. Obviously that kind of perfection (as far as *creation* is concerned) which is consistent with growth and development is a higher kind of perfection than that which is static and final. For the higher perfection belongs to the realm of life. A Christian is not a statue, nor is he the product of a carpenter; he is alive. True Christian perfection makes normal growth possible, not needless.

The image of Christ. Not only is the nature of the divine provision in the New Testament covenant seen in the *remedial terms* used and their *modifiers,* but in an even more profound and conclusive sense it is seen in the fact that Christlikeness in heart is the privilege (as well as the earnest desire) of the believer. The rectification of man's nature in *regeneration* and *entire sanctification* is that man might be conformed to the *image of Christ.* So says Paul in Rom. 8:29, wherein the great, grand sweep of the redemptive purpose is delineated. We are purified, circumcised, sanctified, made perfect, in order that we might be like Jesus. This is the grand objective of the divine economy in establishing the Kingdom among fallen men.

But we must clearly distinguish between image and stature. In Eph. 4:13, Paul admonishes the church to grow that it might attain to the measure of the *stature* of Christ. That is an ultimate goal. But to be conformed inwardly to the *image* of Christ is an immediate privilege through grace. This image consists of two elements, first the *mind of Christ*. "Let this mind be in you, which was also in Christ Jesus," Paul admonishes the Philippians (2:5). This refers to the frame of mind, or the disposition, which prompted Jesus to divest himself of His heavenly powers, and become not only a Man but a Servant, a Servant "obedient unto death, even the death of the cross." If we are conformed to the image of Christ in this sense, then we no longer desire chiefly to be served, but to serve. We no longer are stubbornly determined to have our own way, and to protect our rights at all costs. Rather we desire to let God have His way in us and through us, even though it means that our natural desires, and even life itself, be expendable.

The second element in the image of Christ is the *affections* which governed the Lord Jesus. Dr. Wiley used to say that one of the deepest things in the Bible about Jesus was the statement in Hebrews (quoted from the Old Testament) that He "loved righteousness, and hated iniquity" (1:9). What a man is in his heart of hearts, in the secret citadel of his being, can be measured by what he loves and hates. Jesus loved His Father with a perfect love and loved righteousness as a corollary of His love for the Father. As a further corollary He hated unrighteousness and iniquity with a perfect hatred. So will we if we are conformed to His image. It is not our profession but our preferences which determine the real quality of our character. What looks good to us, what appeals to us, what is attractive to us? A holy person will find within himself a growing revulsion toward wickedness and evil wherever he sees it, in whatever form he finds it. It is this which will prompt him to turn off some radio or TV programs, to reject some magazines, to lay aside some books, to refrain from some places. He will do it not out of a sense of duty or loyalty only to his denomination, but out of a deep inner compulsion of his own spirit. He will find evil profoundly repugnant, just as he finds holiness and righteousness profoundly attractive.

This *image* is our privilege now. It was exemplified by Paul himself, who counted "all things but loss for the excellency of the knowledge of Christ Jesus," his Lord (Phil. 3:8). It was exemplified by Timothy, who was like-minded (Phil. 2:19-20). The Philippians themselves were exhorted to let the mind of Christ prevail in them (2:5). Have we been conformed in our inner *motivation* and in the governing *affections* of our being to the image of the Lord Jesus?

SUMMARY

1. The New Covenant (Testament) speaks to us of a new power for holiness through Christ, our Saviour, who gives to the Church the Holy Spirit for the accomplishment within individual believers of their personal renovation.

2. While there are elements of truth in the idea of suppression, as also in the idea of counteraction, neither term is scriptural when used as designating God's way of dealing with indwelling sin. On the contrary, as the remedial terms used in the Bible show, God's purpose is to remove sin from the heart; and as the modifying terms indicate, He desires that this removal shall be thorough and complete, in this life.

3. This is not the removal of our dependence on the aid of the Holy Spirit, nor does it make either sin or backsliding impossible. It does mean the removal of the bent to willfulness and disloyalty which makes consistent holiness impossible.

4. To be wholly sanctified is not finality in spiritual growth, but rather the beginning of normal growth. One is wholly sanctified in the sense that he is *entirely* "on the altar," *entirely* yielded at the very center of his

being, *entirely* resting in the cleansing Blood, and *entirely* possessed by the Holy Spirit within.

5. To be "perfect" is to be full of love, with no mixture of hate or any other passion or motive contrary to love. It does not mean to be free from mistakes and weaknesses.

6. The real aim is that we might be like Christ. We may be conformed *now* to His image in the sense of disposition to serve and obey God at all costs, and in the further sense of loving righteousness and hating iniquity. But all our lives we will be becoming *more* like Him in our strength of character and outward personality. The inward image and the outward stature are not the same.

QUESTIONS FOR FURTHER DISCUSSION

1. How does the Redeemer deal with the defilement of the "sons of Levi," according to Mal. 3:3? What Bible type of the Holy Spirit is suggested here? Is this a deeper cleansing agent than water?

2. Is there any real difference between the meanings of *purify* and *eradicate?*

3. In the analogy of the cleansed leper it was suggested that the healed man might still have to go through life minus an arm or a foot, or in other ways carry with him the scars of his past disease. But in the illustration of the half-renovated house (p. 65) it was insisted that the "deep stains" must be removed. Is there inconsistency here?

4. What is the difference between "acquired depravity," which is cleansed in regeneration (called *initial sanctification*), and "inherited depravity," which is cleansed in entire sanctification?

CHAPTER FIVE

The Divine Plan of Realization

Scriptures for background:
   Matt. 3:1-12; Luke 24:36-49; John 14:15-18; John 17:15-23; Acts 1:8; Acts 2:1-39; Acts 15:6-9

It is more important that Christians be personally victorious than that they be professionally successful or publicly brilliant. Saintliness will go farther than ability. The ongoing influence of men such as John Wesley is sustained more by what they were than by what they did. Personal failures and inconsistencies, on the other hand, if persistent and glaring, tend to dissipate a man's influence. As a result his public skill is dissolved in the acids of lost confidence. And the more prominent and talented a Christian is, the more devastating is his personal failure in its disastrous consequences.

Therefore the "power" which should most concern the Christian is the power to be triumphantly holy. We have already seen that true victory must be measured in terms of perfect love, and that this will never be the consistent experience of a Christian as long as he is in a double-minded state. We have also seen that God has provided something better than the carnal state for His children, and that this includes a complete eradication of the sinful principle from the human heart. As far as sin is concerned, God's plan is neither suppression nor counteraction but cleansing. We have seen this in our study of the terms used in the New Testament describing the cleansing and correcting power of the blood of Jesus, as applied by the Holy Spirit.

But how are we personally to experience this deliverance? How is it to be brought about? By what means are believers to be purified? When and how are they to be sanctified wholly? These are the questions which we must attempt to answer in this chapter. We have seen that God has planned a second work of grace. Now we must inquire still more carefully: Is this second work of grace to be a distinct crucial experience, knowable and dateable, or a gradual change in the soul over a period of many years? Further, is a second work of grace a necessity or merely an option in the realization of the divine provision? Is it invariably God's plan? If so, why? Again, what is the nature of this second work of grace and how is it realized?

Not everything is done in regeneration which needs to be done. If Christians are to be cleansed of indwelling sin, it obviously must be after conversion. In this sense there can no problem arise concerning the term "second." But even though *second,* it might still be a slow, quiet, almost imperceptible inward change accomplished by the Holy Spirit through growth in grace, spurred by the wear and tear of everyday life. That there *is* gradual growth all along the Christian life is unquestionably true, but the amount of growth before a definite experience of entire sanctification is usually very small.

THE BAPTISM WITH THE SPIRIT

However, the most satisfactory way of settling the issue of crisis versus gradualness is to see that God's provision in Christ for the remedy of man's sinful nature is inseparably associated with the experience for believers known as the baptism with the Holy Spirit. If we can understand the Scripture concerning this baptism, everything else will fall naturally into place. Let us therefore see what the Scripture says.

The promise of this baptism. This promise was clearly enunciated by John the Baptist. His statement is of sufficient importance and significance to be found in all three of the Synoptic Gospels. Matthew expresses it like this, "I indeed baptize you with water unto repentance: but he that cometh after me is mightier than I, whose shoes I am not worthy to bear: he shall baptize you with the Holy Ghost, and with fire" (3:11). Just as John baptizes persons in or with water, so Jesus is to baptize persons in or with the Holy Spirit. As John is the agent in the first baptism, so Jesus is the Agent in the Spirit baptism. Man can baptize with water but only the Lord himself can baptize with the Holy Spirit. This makes it easy to see that, whereas John's baptism is visible and physical, our Lord's baptism with the Holy Spirit is invisible and spiritual. It is none the less experiential and personally knowable.

Furthermore, as water is the *medium* of the first baptism, so is it also a symbol or picture. It pictures the cleansing of the life from the guilt of the past and the practice of sins in the present. It symbolizes also the induction of the repentant believer into a new relationship with God known as the new birth. Water is thus an outward sign of an inward work. But the symbol of the Spirit-baptism is *fire,* which suggests inward purity, warmth, and power. This too speaks of a definite and crucial induction or initiation, this time into an *advanced* relationship with God, or a new level of religious experience.

It is important to see further that this promised baptism with the Holy Spirit is not the same as the birth of the Spirit, about which Jesus talked to Nicodemus, which constitutes the essential gateway into the kingdom of God. In that discussion (John 3:1-13) a different preposition is used in the Greek. In speaking of the new birth it is proper to speak of birth *of* or *by* the Spirit, since the Spirit himself is the Agent who quickens the repentant sinner into spiritual life. Spiritual life has its *origin* in the Spirit, just as physical life has its origin in the flesh (v. 6). Such is the sense of the Greek preposition here. But when speaking of the Spirit-baptism which John promised, it is not proper to use the preposition *of* or *by,* for Jesus is the Agent and the Spirit is the *medium,* just as water is the medium in John's baptism. We may say therefore that in the Spirit-baptism Jesus "pours" the Spirit upon us and inducts us into the *full life of the Spirit.* In the birth of the Spirit we have the beginning of spiritual life, but in the baptism with the Spirit we have the flowering or fullness of spiritual life. This fulfills the Old Testament promise and also characterizes the New Testament standard.

The fulfillment of the promise. The careful student of the New Testament cannot fail to see that John the Baptist's promise was fulfilled on the Day of Pentecost and in repetitions of that experience thereafter. If what occurred on the Day of Pentecost was not the baptism with the Holy Spirit as promised by John, then John's promise was never fulfilled, for there is no other religious occurrence recorded in the New Testament which even approximates in power and depth that which occurred on the Day of Pentecost. Yet the Book of Acts does not use the term "baptism," but other terms such as "filled," and "came upon them," and "poured out," when telling of the coming of the Holy Spirit. This would indicate very clearly that these are synonymous and interchangeable terms. To be "baptized with the Spirit" and to have the Holy Spirit "come upon" one are one and the same experience.

Furthermore it is perfectly clear that the inspired writer of Acts sees in the events of Pentecost the clear fulfillment both of the Old Testament prophecies which describe the new covenant in Christ and of *the promise* which John first enunciated. Note that this promise was repeated on various occasions by Jesus himself. Best of all, Peter makes it clear that this *promise* and this *fulfillment* (which is to say, the baptism with the Holy Spirit) were not for the apostles only, but are the privilege of all God's children in all generations. He says, "For the promise is unto you, and to your children, and to all that are afar off, even as many as the Lord our God shall call" (Acts 2:39). This reaches down to our generation and takes us all in—yes, even you and me.

There can be little question, either, but that the events of Pentecost were not only the fulfillment of John's promise, but of our Lord's promise in the Upper Room to send to His disciples another Comforter, the Holy Spirit, that He might abide with them forever (John 14:15-18, 26; 15:26; 16:7-15). This gift of the Spirit was to be an inward relationship and an inward fullness by which the disciples were to be made strong, and by which they were to become effective as witnesses of the Lord Jesus, fulfilling yet another promise, "But you will receive power when the Holy Spirit comes upon you" (Acts 1:8, NEB). The Holy Spirit thus *indwelling the believers* in His fullness as Comforter would (1) help them with their infirmities (Rom. 8:26), (2) reveal Christ to them (John 16:14), (3) teach them and guide them (John 14:26; 16:13), (4) produce in others round about them conviction of sin, righteousness, and judgment (John 16:8), and (5) enable them to witness for Christ by word and life courageously and effectively (Acts 1:8).

This baptism identifiable as entire sanctification. Many questions may arise in our minds at this point, but one thing only is important to make clear right now, and that is that all of the rich blessings which were to attend the gift of the Holy Spirit were abundantly and fully realized by the disciples themselves. There was no disappointment, no need to modify expectations or apologize for failure. On the contrary, God accomplished in them that which was exceeding abundantly above all that they could ask or think according to the power that was working in them (Eph. 3:20). There were marvelous qualities which characterized them immediately and fully: the bursting forth of spiritual vitality, the pushing back of the horizons, the sudden spiritual understanding and insight, the deliverance from the paralyzing fears and tensions, the perfect unity of spirit and fellowship, the clear-eyed, purehearted, undivided allegiance to Jesus Christ, the calm courage in public identification, the buoyancy of spirit in facing peril and loss, the disregard of all selfish consideration. There was no exception in respect to anyone recorded in the Book of the Acts who genuinely and definitely experienced this Spirit-baptism. Who would care to deny that there was a breathtakingly marvelous transformation in the disciples themselves? A cowardly Peter before the maid became a courageous preacher before the multitude. Those who once bickered over who should be the greatest now rejoiced that they were counted worthy to suffer shame for His name. Such changes constituted the great miracle of Pentecost!

This leads us directly to the implied promise in the prayer of our Lord for His disciples: "Sanctify them through thy truth: thy word is truth" (John 17:17).[1] This, too, obviously found its fulfillment on the Day of Pentecost. The word of *promise* and the word of *command* which prompted the disciples to tarry for ten days in Jerusalem became the word of *power* as the Holy Spirit came upon them and did exactly what Jesus had prayed should be done—sanctify them. If we are to separate entire sanctification from the baptism with the Holy Spirit then we must ask: When was Jesus' prayer for the sanctification of the disciples fulfilled? When we study the transformation in the disciples and read the Book of Acts, we cannot but answer: The promise of John the Baptist and the prayer of Jesus the Saviour were fulfilled *at precisely the same time and were but different aspects of the one experience.* A modern Pentecostalist once said, "The holiness people have missed Pentecost and the Pentecostal people have missed holiness." But that is impossible. True Pentecost includes holiness and true holiness is impossible without Pentecost. When men are sanctified wholly they are baptized with the Holy Spirit, and when they are baptized with the Holy Spirit they are sanctified wholly. One includes and implies the other.

A SECOND, DISTINCT WORK

As far as the recipients on the Day of Pentecost were concerned this was obviously a second experience.

[1] The prayer that the Father would "sanctify" the disciples is voiced in the aorist tense. While this tense does not of itself prove an instantaneous work, it proves a definite and *completed* work, and cannot be construed to imply a gradual sanctifying which is never completed; therefore the fulfillment by a crisis experience such as at Pentecost is strongly implied. But in v. 19 an even stronger tense is used: ". . . they may be sanctified" is in the perfect tense, clearly expressing our Lord's intention that they shall be brought into a *state* of sanctification, definitely accomplished and continuously maintained.

Those 120 who were filled with the Holy Spirit were all fervent believers and true disciples of the Lord Jesus. This was not the beginning of their spiritual life, but their elevation to a new plane of spiritual life.

Only believers eligible. After the Day of Pentecost, also, baptism with the Holy Spirit was an experience for which only believers were eligible. There is not one instance in the Book of Acts of Spirit-infilling where there is not evidence of some measure of *prior* spiritual life. This is true not only of the original disciples and apostles, but of the Samaritans, of Paul himself, and of the Ephesian believers. Even Cornelius and his household are not an exception. Admittedly their knowledge was limited, and they needed clear instruction concerning the saviourhood of Jesus. But the record is perfectly clear that Cornelius was a devout man prior to being baptized with the Holy Spirit. He is spoken of as "one that feared God with all his house, which gave much alms to the people, and prayed to God alway" (Acts 10:2). Furthermore Peter acknowledged him as "accepted" with God (v. 35), and even more significantly, called attention to the fact that he *already had heard the gospel* (vv. 36-37). Any confusion or uncertainty in their minds concerning Jesus and Jesus alone as the basis of the forgiveness of their sins was cleared up in Peter's sermon. Upon this being cleared up they were instantly eligible for the exact experience which the apostles themselves received on the Day of Pentecost. When Peter later related the events in the Cornelius household, he identified what they received as the same as what the apostles received. Significantly, its essential feature in his mind was not the speaking with tongues but the *purification of their hearts* (15:9). It is clear that Cornelius was entirely sanctified (made holy in heart) when he was baptized with the Spirit, and was baptized with the Spirit when he was sanctified. It always works this way. But the main consideration at the moment is that this experience was not received by Cornelius without a foundation of some measure of previous spiritual life.

This fact of *secondness,* which is so obvious in the Book of Acts, fits in with the basic principle stated by Jesus in His promise in the Upper Room: ". . . whom the world cannot receive, because it seeth him not, neither knoweth him." This suggests that the gift of the Spirit, by which is meant the indwelling of the Holy Spirit in His fullness, cannot be received at the time of repentance and regeneration. At that point one is not yet qualified. One must first *qualify* for the gift of the Holy Spirit by ceasing to belong to the world and beginning to belong to Jesus Christ. Once having entered into a saving relationship with Jesus Christ, one begins to possess the privileges and the prerogatives of such discipleship. And the chief privilege and prerogative is the promise of the indwelling Holy Spirit as *Paraclete* (Comforter).

Reasons for "secondness." But the idea of a second crisis as a *necessary* stage in experiencing full salvation may still be a problem to some people. Why does not God baptize with the Spirit simultaneously with the birth of the Spirit? Why are believers not regenerated and entirely sanctified at the same time? It is clear that in actual fact this is not the case, but some inquiring mind may still persist with the "why?" Possibly at this point in our study, therefore, we may wisely point out that not only is the doctrine of the second work of grace clearly substantiated in biblical history, as we have seen by our study of the Book of Acts, but that it is *perfectly rational.*

1. For one thing, the element of *crisis* is inescapable. A little later on we will discuss the necessity of faith for sanctification as the divinely appointed condition for the realization of this experience. But faith implies a crisis; for what we must believe for, we believe for *now.*

Otherwise faith is not perfect; it is merely the faith of expectation rather than appropriation. Furthermore, the *unitary* nature of indwelling sin requires complete and immediate action on the part of the Holy Spirit if it is to be eliminated. In our humanity we may strive to kill the monster of sin piecemeal, by striking off first this tentacle and then that. But it does not work that way. God's method is to deal decisively and crucially with *self-willfulness* itself. We may work for a while on jealousy, or possibly pride or anger, but all of these sins are but manifestations of a hidden, deep, underlying *unsurrendered self*. When that enemy is slain, the tentacles loosen their hold.

Furthermore, gradualness alone is not compatible with what we know about either God or ourselves as Christians. Gradualness is not compatible with the will of God that we be holy now, or the power of God to make us holy now. Gradualness is not compatible with the hunger and thirst after righteousness experienced by a convicted believer who wants immediate release. Then, many scholars have placed considerable emphasis on the fact that gradualness is not compatible with the use of the aorist tense in the Greek (the tense of completed action), used so significantly in verbs relating to the sanctification of the believer.

2. Furthermore the sinner's personal sins and acquired depravity, for which he alone is responsible, must be cleared away before the deeper problem of inherited disposition can be dealt with (cf. Matt. 18:3). A restoration to spiritual life and sonship, involving the cessation of estrangement and rebellion, is logically the prerequisite for the correction of a racial fault, a fault which is not the sinner's own doing, but his heritage from Adam (Acts 2:38). The two phases of redemption available in this life, justification and entire sanctification—the pardon of personal sins and the purging of in-

herited sinfulness—are so momentous in themselves, and so profoundly different, that the accomplishment of both in a single religious experience would be highly improbable as a characteristic norm in the divine plan.

3. But these are theological considerations. There are ethical and psychological considerations also which strengthen the case. *The importance of the human response and cooperation at every stage must be kept always in view as we study the divine plan of realization.* God does not perform His works of grace in our sleep. The ethical nature of true holiness demands human cooperation. One of the objections given by disbelievers in a crisis experience is, "Can ethical character be imparted by a stroke of omnipotence?" Certainly not by an arbitrary, one-sided stroke. God imparts holiness only to the degree that one is ready to receive holiness. God's processes of redemption must proceed in step with man's readiness. The blessings of salvation are not bestowed on nonparticipating recipients. *Prevenient*[2] grace may be unconditionally operative, but not saving grace. God demands that we *ask* if we are to receive, and that we exercise faith if we are to experience. These are conscious, deliberate acts, involving a sense of need, of deep desire, and deliberate choice and decision. Man's moral agency is thus respected in every step of vital personal redemption.

The truth is, the sinner does not see his deep racial depravity. Neither does a joyous, happy, newborn child of God see his further need. But he must see it if he is to intelligently seek heart holiness. There must be a sense of need or there cannot be a sense of fulfillment. And if God is going to cleanse the heart of the carnal mind, it must be only upon the definite decision and

---

[2]A term meaning the grace of God operating in human hearts *before* repentance and saving faith. The word means "going before."

choice of the subject. The race could not have been afflicted with this fatal disease without man's choice; neither can there be healing without man's choice. *It is this personal choice which keeps the transaction on an ethical plane.* If God were content with a nonethical holiness, He could bestow His works of grace irrespective of our readiness or cooperation. But since it is ethical holiness which God wants, it must be holiness which is desired, chosen, sought, appropriated by faith, and continuously confirmed by daily obedience.

This is not to deny the fact that there may be a time lapse, of a greater or less extent, in the process of entering into a satisfactory experience of the baptism with the Holy Spirit. This may be due to our own ignorance or possibly our stubbornness. A series of humiliating and shameful defeats may be required to produce a ripened and intensified desperation.

Then the crisis itself may involve several sub-crises before a satisfactory consummation is reached. An experience can be crucial in the sense that its beginning and ending occur within a definite period of time, yet within this period of time there may be stages. These stages cannot be construed as individual works of grace, but as stages (though unnecessary) in the one work of grace. The waffle iron did not work properly one morning and it took about one hour for us to get through the breakfast. We "enjoyed" it by piecemeal. Yet we could not say that we had three or four breakfasts. We had only one. To relate this again to Pentecost, we must remind ourselves that we do not speak of the year of Pentecost, but the day. A young man who had been up-and-down in his Christian experience was heard to pray, "Lord, put me where I'll stay put." And the prayer proved to be a turning point in his life. That was the climax of an "extended crisis," but it was a climax which was definite, memorable, and satisfactory.

But this gets us back to a simple fact of experience: indwelling sin, or inbred sin, is not removed at conversion but still remains. It remained in the disciples even after they forsook all to follow Jesus. It remained in the Corinthians even after they had been saved out of gross paganism and were babes in Christ. It remained in you and me. And so agree all of the major denominational creeds. Therefore if inbred sin is ever to be removed it must be as a second work of grace. Inbred sin *is* removed in entire sanctification. And since entire sanctification is experienced in the baptism with the Holy Spirit, and since the baptism with the Holy Spirit is the privilege of every child of God *right now,* it is apparent that God's plan of realization is a definite experience which is immediately available to all who need it and who sufficiently desire it.

On Long Island a young woman was radiantly converted and at once began telling her friends—in fact, almost all whom she met—what God had done for her. To please her husband she went to certain worldly places which before her conversion she had frequented without thought. Now, upon returning home, she said simply, "Honey, those places are not for me!" About three weeks after her conversion her pastor felt strongly impressed to call on her. She greeted him with a torrent of words: "I'm glad you came. Last Sunday you said something about an inward warfare. I've had a war on the inside alright. This morning in prayer the Lord showed me I must put my husband on the altar. The Lord is talking to me about my little girl, but I'm not so sure about her. But I prayed, 'Lord, I must have more, if I am to go on! Yet I don't want to go back—I'm ashamed of that! Lord, send the preacher today to help me!'" Then she burst out with the question, "How long must I wait before I can be sanctified?" They prayed, but she was not quite satisfied.

The next night she came to the church altar, and in a few moments her face was aglow with a heavenly radiance such as is seldom seen. It was bathed in glory. She said: "Now I know I have surrendered to Him completely." And she was at rest. But in this crisis she entered into an intimate relationship with her Lord of which she would not have been capable three weeks before when she came as a sin-stained rebel seeking pardon. Her inner being was united in single-minded confirmation of her new allegiance. There was nothing left in her that wanted to go back, or even drag its feet. She was wholly the Lord's and thus holy within. She had been entirely sanctified by the baptism with the Holy Spirit.

Summary

1. *The promise* of the Holy Spirit, as related to the advanced privileges of this dispensation, is seen to be the baptism with the Spirit, as promised by John, and this experience is seen to be available only to believers in the Lord Jesus. It is thus a second definite work of grace.

2. The fulfillment of our Lord's prayer for the *sanctification* of the disciples, His promise of *power,* and the bestowing of the promised *gift* of the Spirit were all simultaneously experienced by believers on the Day of Pentecost, and in similar baptisms with the Spirit thereafter. Therefore entire sanctification and the baptism with the Spirit are but two aspects of the one experience.

3. God's plan in accomplishing "full salvation" from sin in two distinct steps seems to be an adaptation to man's capacity to see his need and to appropriate grace. It is also due to the ethical nature of salvation, and an expression of God's respect for human choice at each stage in redemption.

4. This is not to depreciate the very great importance of the day-by-day processes of redemption, but it

is to recognize that there are certain basic crisis experiences which sinners must experience in being fully saved without which the processes will be incomplete and unsatisfactory.

5. More emphasis must be placed on the crises than on the processes for the simple reason that human nature dislikes crises and will do everything possible to avoid them. This is true both with the sinner who needs to repent and a believer who needs to consecrate and tarry for purity and power. Therefore both classes need much urging and even warning to press them to action.

Questions for Discussion

1. Why is there usually not much real spiritual progress before one is sanctified wholly?

2. When does one *receive* the Holy Spirit—in the new birth, or in the second work of grace, or in both?

3. If it is not possible for God to sanctify wholly until the believer sees his needs and seeks the blessing, is it possible for the believer to remain saved if he sees his need and refuses to seek in all earnestness?

CHAPTER SIX

The Faith That Sanctifies

Scriptures for background:

Mark 5:22-36; Acts 26:15-18; Rom. 5:1-5; 15:4-13; Gal. 3:1-14.

Faith is mysterious and difficult for many Christians. To some it seems like mere wishful thinking, or fervent hoping—a desperate attempt to "kid" yourself into believing something that in your heart you do not really believe at all. It thus seems like a form of self-deception or self-hypnotism. The little boy expressed this attitude when he explained that faith was "believing what you know ain't so."

When we compare this notion of faith with the biblical insistence that faith is indispensable to salvation, we realize that true faith must be altogether different from wishful thinking. Then when we proceed to read that "without faith it is impossible to please" God (Heb. 11:6), and such declarations of Jesus as "According to your faith be it unto you" (Matt. 9:29), and "All things are possible to him that believeth" (Mark 9:23), we are forced to conclude that we had better find out—fast—what Christian faith is, and have a lot of it.

THE NATURE OF CHRISTIAN FAITH

Trust in God. It would be impossible in such a brief book as this to examine the philosophy of faith thoroughly. But it is important that we see one all-embracing truth: Christian faith begins with belief in a personal God, the God revealed in our Lord Jesus Christ. We have already quoted the opening part of Heb. 11:6; but notice the first clearly specified essential of this faith without which we cannot please God: "He that cometh to God must believe that he is . . ." To doubt the existence of God is naturally to make saving faith imposible—indeed, to detroy all religion.

1. The first plank of Christian faith therefore is the belief in a God big enough to justify my faith, a God who is the Source of all things. The importance of this can be seen by a simple illustration. Walking across the room and flipping the light switch is an act of faith. But that which makes the act effectual is not the faith but an objective fact: the fact that out there somewhere is an electric power plant. There is a real source of power. Without this my act would be mere make-believe. I would accomplish nothing. It is the *fact of God* which keeps faith from being merely a subjective, psychological trick played on oneself. It is the fact of an adequate electrical system which makes turning a switch a rational act. If there were nothing but the switch, turning it with any expectation of results would be both irrational and unscientific. If there were no God, Christian faith would be just as irrational and unscientific. But Christian faith can never be charged with being unscientific or unreasonable unless it can be proved that there is no God.

It must never be forgotten that Christian faith is first and foremost *in God;* it is not faith in *faith.* Suppose a primitive New Guinea highlander learned to flip a switch but knew nothing about the power plant. His faith would be in the switch, and in that case it would be superstition. As long as the power plant was there anyway, whether he knew it or not, he would get the same results and his knowledge or ignorance wouldn't make much difference. But if he managed somehow to detach the switch and reverently take it back to his native land packed neatly in a little box, he would soon discover that in placing his faith in the switch he was placing his faith in the wrong object. So our faith likewise is a form of superstition if it is in faith itself, or in ourselves, or in our church, or in our religious ceremonies, or anything other than, or in detachment from, God himself.

2. The second plank of Christian faith is this: Not only does God exist, but He is trustworthy. Go back to Heb. 11:6: "He that cometh to God must believe that he is, and that he is a rewarder of them that diligently seek him." Thus Christian faith makes an affirmation about God's character. It stakes all on the assumption that God is good. When we combine plank one with plank two we have *trust.* When we once see this, we will see why unbelief is sin. It is a libel on God's character. Unbelief says, "God is not true"; faith says, "God is true, and I will trust Him though He slay me."

Faith the conditional factor. Now in matter of religion God is not only the Power Plant, but the Designer and Creator of the whole system—including the switch. He has set up an arrangement whereby everything depends on the "Company" but *the turning of that switch.* But without that act there can be no light, for that act closes the circuit and releases the current into the lamp.

1. We may say then that the action of the switch is the last link in a chain of causes. The desired effect or

result is *light* in the soul of man, whether the light of pardon or the light of purity. The *basic* causes (or sources) have been provided by God, unconditionally. Theologians sometimes speak of the love of God as the *originating* cause of this light (John 3:16); the *Word* of God as the *instrumental* cause (Jas. 1:21;[1] I Cor. 4:15; John 17:17); the *blood of Jesus* as the *procuring* cause (Rom. 5:6-11; Heb. 13:12); and the Holy Spirit as the *efficient Cause* (I Pet. 1:2). The *system* is perfect, complete, and adequate. But without the turning of the switch there will still be darkness. Faith is this switch. Therefore it is logical for theologians to speak of *faith* as the *conditional* cause of our salvation (Rom. 10:8-10). The power lines of a great city may be humming with current, but it will be of no avail if the occupant of a particular house chooses to remain in darkness. It has been (until now) up to the power company to provide the facilities and the current. Now it is up to the occupant. Similarly all the marvelous provision of salvation through God the Father, Son, and Holy Spirit depends for its efficiency on an act of faith on the part of the "consumer." Without faith the grace of God is blocked at the threshold.

2. There is sound reason why personal salvation must hinge in the final issue on the sinner himself. Only this arrangement makes salvation ethical rather than arbitrary and coercive. By ethical we mean that it is a salvation based on moral foundations. It is a salvation which is offered to man as a moral being—a free agent—rather than imposed on him mechanically as if he were a mere machine. Salvation imposed on man by the unconditional action of the Spirit would have no moral value, since it would not be man's choice. There are moral meaning and true obligation in a marriage entered into freely and willingly by both parties. But if the girl

[1]Cf. Phillips, RSV, and NEB versions. Cf. also Jas. 1:18.

is drugged and forced into marriage against her will, the union cannot possibly be consummated on a moral basis. This would be an unethical arrangement—indeed, a monstrous crime. God doesn't "save" that way. He woos, but will not force. Therefore a conditional factor, dependent on man, must be basic to the divine plan of salvation.

3. There are not only sound reasons why there should be such a conditional factor, but sound reasons also why this conditional factor should be faith. For one thing, in final analysis, the condition would have to be either faith or works, or a combination of faith and works. There are three possibilities.

a. Man must save himself apart from Calvary. This is *works* alone.

b. Man must merit or earn *part* of his salvation. That is, what God has done in Christ must be supplemented and completed by something man does, perhaps works of penance, or acquiring a certain level of goodness, or maybe a certain level of knowledge, or making large gifts of money. This is works *and* faith.

c. Or He must just accept this salvation God has provided. This is the method of simple faith, and it is the Christian way. Any condition other than faith would at once exclude the mass of men. But faith is within the reach of all. It is, furthermore, a *moral* basis for a reconciliation, for it is a full, unreserved acceptance of the Word of God and the sufficiency of the Blood atonement. It assumes that God is true, therefore honors God. Man's act of faith thus becomes the first truly righteous act he can perform, and the foundation for all subsequent righteousness. "Abraham believed God, and it was counted unto him for righteousness" (Rom. 4:3). Any form of works whatsoever—even supposing that we are saved by our tears—is an attempt to add to the work of Christ, and thus is a detraction from the sufficiency of the salvation God provides in Him.

4. Faith is both an *act* and an *attitude*. As an act it is a decision to believe; as an attitude it is a habitual trust and commitment. It is a voluntary act of man, yet not without the aid of the Holy Spirit, and not without meeting certain secondary conditions imposed by faith itself.

5. Perfect faith includes four essential elements: (a) *Intellectual assent* to the truth (Rom. 10:17; Mark 1:15; II Tim. 2:25). (b) *Personal commitment* to the truth (John 1:37; II Thess. 2:13). The first involves the mind; the second involves the will. The truth demands not only our assent but our surrender. (c) *Open confession* (Rom. 10:10). What we believe we are willing to acknowledge. Hesitancy here will prove that either we are not fully convinced or not fully committed. (d) *Appropriate action,* which is obedience (I Pet. 1:22). True faith always impels action. Abraham believed the word of God, and it was accounted unto him for righteousness. But he *proved* his faith by prompt obedience in offering up Isaac. "Faith without works is dead" (Jas. 2:26).

FAITH AND SANCTIFICATION

It has long been held in evangelical circles that we are justified by faith alone. But it is not always clearly seen that faith is the key to our sanctification as well. Because many factors enter into the alteration of our character, such as natural maturing and development, self-discipline, sorrow, and pain, we are apt to suppose that these are the sanctifying agents. It is easy therefore for a new convert who was forgiven by faith to proceed to try to achieve sanctification by works. But these various contributing factors are but the raw materials which the Holy Spirit uses in bringing about the change of our character. The real Agent is the Holy Spirit, and it is our faith which turns the Holy Spirit loose in our souls. It is as we believe that He is able to use the raw materials of life to our profit. Unbelief will block the Holy Spirit, and as a result the advantages of time and learning and age and experience will be forfeited.

Our sanctification in this broad general sense depends on faith in a still more particular respect. The Spirit's ability to sanctify continuously depends on His action in sanctifying definitely and specifically in a second work of grace. And this definite experience, which is sometimes called "the second blessing," is as much dependent on our faith as any other phase of our full salvation.

This truth carries certain corollaries:

1. *Our faith must be in Jesus and Jesus alone.* We must see that Christ died to sanctify us as well as justify us (John 17:19; Eph. 5:25-26; Heb. 13:12). We must pin our faith totally in the atoning Blood as the ground of our holiness. Purification of the heart must be seen as the action of the Spirit made possible at the Cross.

2. *Our faith must be in Jesus specifically for entire sanctification*—not something else or something less.[2] Indefinite faith will produce an indefinite experience and an indefinite testimony. Here again it is true: "according to your faith be it unto you." Timid faith that believes only for "a closer walk with God," or "a little more power," or "a blessing," falls short of that necessary boldness and definiteness which lays hold of the promises for a perfect cleansing and complete infilling.

3. *Our faith must become perfect.* By this is meant it must have in it the four essential elements which we

[2]Acts 8:15; 9:17; 19:6; 26:18. Cf. Matt. 8:2, where the leper's faith was specific. Now read again Matt. 9:29, together with Mark 10:51.

have listed above: (*a*) We must be convinced that Christ can sanctify, and is willing to do so (the assent of the mind). (*b*) We must submit totally to Christ for sanctification, including its full implications (the surrender of our will). (*c*) We must believe that Christ does sanctify us now, on the authority of His Word, the certainty of His integrity, and the basis of the Blood, because we have asked in obedient faith. And we must affirm this faith openly—not testifying to our feelings but to our faith (open confession). (*d*) We must act our faith, even when feelings seem to contradict it.

But lest the seeker deceive himself by a false faith which brings no change or blessing, it is necessary now to discuss more particularly the "works" of faith in relation to entire sanctification.

The Prerequisites of Sanctifying Faith

When we talk about the prerequisites of faith we mean those conditions which the seeker must meet if true faith is going to be possible. Faith must be morally structured. It can exist only in a context of complete honesty and obedience. Actually these conditions are more than "contexts." They are part of the warp and woof of faith itself; they are the "works" which proceed from faith as its validation, and in some sense precede faith. But having already rejected "works" as a means of salvation, it may seem confusing, to say the least, now to drag them back in. It is necessary therefore to stop long enough to see if we can distinguish between the works which Paul rejects in Romans and which James affirms in his Epistle.

The "works" of faith. "Works" as a means of achieving holiness, or of earning or meriting salvation, we have already seen to be inconsistent with simple faith, and a reflection on the adequacy of Jesus as Saviour. "Works" in this sense implies that we and the Lord are joint saviours, a sort of team in achieving eternal life.

But there is another kind of "works" demanded by the nature of simple faith itself, as an essential element of faith. A friend said that as a boy he and a pal were in a country store at the Christmas season, when the proprietor called to them. Holding out a shiny, red, toy fire truck, he said, "Here, I'm giving this to you as a Christmas present." My friend held back in suspicion and disbelief, his hands behind him. The other boy took the prize, and with shining eyes walked out of the store and went home. In the one boy we see unbelief acting. In the other boy we see faith acting. To have stood back and still professed to believe absolutely in the storekeeper's offer would have been contradictory. *Receiving* was the work of faith, which proved faith real. Yet it was not the kind of "work" which in any sense bought, earned, or merited the gift!

Where there is genuine faith there is always suitable action—or at least the faith will accomplish nothing if separated from its suitable action. It may be possible for a seasoned traveler to have faith in a certain airplane and still choose not to go. But in this case his faith is dead; it gets him nowhere. If his faith is going to accomplish anything, he must secure a ticket and get on the plane. In the matter of salvation, the "ticket" has already been purchased for us. But it will not get us to heaven if we do not avail ourselves of it—and *on the purchase terms.* Thus does faith imply "works" in the sense that James discusses the question.

The work of surrender. The fundamental work without which faith is spurious is *surrender.* This is true at all stages of the Christian life, whether conversion, entire sanctification, or any subsequent crisis. Surrender is the submission of our wills to the lordship of Jesus. It is an unreserved and uncompromising yes to His terms, whether they be small or large.

In the first work of grace—the new birth—this surrender takes the form of *repentance.* It is a surrender of our sins. It is a cessation of our rebellion and a renunciation of the old life. It is an acceptance of Christ's claims upon us, and an adoption of His standards for our lives. But in the second salvation crisis our surrender takes the direction of *consecration*. It is not our love of sin and the world we are giving up, but our love of ourselves. In repentance we abandon the *bad*, but in consecration we surrender the *good*. This touches our inherent right to ourselves. This is not dealing with evil practices but with God's gifts. "Why should we give them up?" we whimper. Yet this and nothing less is the biblical challenge: "I beseech you therefore, brethren, by the mercies of God, that ye present your bodies a living sacrifice, holy, acceptable unto God, which is your reasonable service" (Rom. 12:1). Most Christians find that it is far easier to give up sins than to give up self. In this struggle the carnal mind feels that God is asking too much.

Seeking and searching. It is for this reason that making a thorough and honest consecration generally requires a little time. Not that any emphasis should ever be placed on the time factor, as if there were any virtue or necessity in so many hours of seeking or so much fasting. But the soul does need a deep view of its own corruption. It does need to count the cost. It does need to specify the items of yielding—money, job, family, ambitions, affections, reputation, success or failure, occupation; the present or the future, the "known bundle" and the "unknown bundle" (as old-timers used to call it). We must genuinely come to grips with practical, personal, down-to-earth issues which bother us. What if God should . . . ? Yes, we must face *that* possibility, until we are able to say, "Not my will, but thine, be done." In this process we see that God's will may cut across the natural. Then the natural must be surrendered. The ego must be slain. The *Big I* must be crucified. This is not the death *of* self, but a deliberate and voluntary death *to* self. The self with all its "rights" must be submerged in God, for the Spirit's unhindered habitation and control.

Unless the seeker gives himself enough time to at least think about these issues, not just in general, but as they affect *him,* he will not have any rational basis for saying, "I am all on the altar."³ That must not be a glibly said shibboleth; it must be an intelligently known fact.

And in this searching, probing, and yielding, adjustments may be revealed which need to be made, not only with God himself, but possibly with men. If sins have been committed since regeneration, they need to be confessed and forgiven. All hindrances need to be cleared away. It could be that God will require apologies or even additional restitution. This is the self-purging which the Bible enjoins (Jas. 4: 7-8; I John 3: 3).

Furthermore, this process is bringing about the disclosure of one's motives in wanting to be sanctified. It is to be feared that some have a desire for holiness that is mixed with selfish ambition. They want the Holy Spirit with a motive that accents the power, because they itch for the advantages such power will bring to them. It is seen as a grand way to exalt self, even while exalting the Lord. Instead of wanting their ego crucified they really want it fed. The prospect of power, with the resulting praise and prestige and honor, seems exciting and inviting. The subtle thing is that often this power motive is half-hidden from the view of the ardent seeker. He has made himself think he wants God, when what he

---

³The Christian's altar is the cross of the Lord Jesus Christ. The phrase is metaphorical, and simply means: "I am surrendered and consecrated completely to Christ." As an expression it is reminiscent of the burnt offering described in the Old Testament (Leviticus 1), the chief characteristic of which was that the *entire* animal was put on the altar and burned as "a sweet savour unto the Lord." Cf. Rom. 12:1.

really wants is God's gifts. And he sees those gifts as a new way to get attention.

One man confessed, "I look after number one"—meaning himself. An entirely consecrated man doesn't say that. What is more, he doesn't practice it. From the moment of genuine surrender and consecration all considerations of prestige, power, advancement, ease, or possessions cease to be determinative factors or goals. In their place life's determinative, all-embracing motive is a desire for the will and glory of God. Secondary motives, such as desire for improved salary and physical comforts or enlarged opportunity, may carry a limited appeal, but they are not finally determinative. We are able to keep them subject to the *master motive*—not with self-pity, either, but gladly. And if such a person once again begins to dance to the tune of these earthly goals and values, and starts playing the "angles" for his own interests, he will be advertising to the world that he is backslidden in heart, because he has basely betrayed the terms of his consecration.

The symbolic picture of consecration is an ox standing patiently and resignedly between an altar on the left and a plow on the right—"for sacrifice or service." This symbolism must become reality or the seeker will have a defective consecration and as a consequence a defective faith. Most people would be glad to be God's *horse,* prancing, high-spirited, noble, and beautiful, admired by all around. But *an ox!*—drab, uninteresting, humble, unnoticed. The idea is repugnant. Then others are willing to consecrate for service but not for sacrifice. They will work hard for the Lord as long as they can keep their comforts and manage the purse strings. Maybe the Lord will let them live in comparative comfort, but the heart must not be tied to material things. Deep down there must be the understanding that they are a bonus from the Lord which He can withdraw at any time. No Christian can live in a fine house and either become sanctified or remain sanctified unless he can look around and say gladly and sincerely: "Lord, this is all on the altar. Thank You for it today. Help me to use it for Thy glory and not hoard it selfishly and nervously. It is at Thy disposal. If You take it from me through adversity, I will still love and serve Thee. If You ask for it I will give it. It is already Thine." Not all are Howard Hamlins, called to give up a successful and lucrative medical practice to go to Africa in middle age, but all are required to be willing. The basic inward consecration must be just as deep and genuine. In most cases this equal consecration will be equally demonstrated by "standing by the stuff" in the hometown and local church as loyal, reliable, spiritual laymen.

The carnal heart in its eel-like slipperiness will seek by every possible rationalization to blunt these demands and soften these issues, and find some sort of compromise. It will look for the easier way. Here is the cutting edge of our Lord's ultimatum: "If any man will come after me, let him deny himself . . ." (Matt. 16:24). This word now speaks with authority. The Christian must refuse to settle for less than total self-crucifixion. Maybe at most points there will be no struggle. Generally however there is at least one sensitive issue, one dearly loved "Isaac," which will wrench the soul. This is what we mean by "dying out." Unless this kind of self-surrender is deep and genuine, faith cannot be perfect, and imperfect faith will not function in releasing the cleansing power of the Holy Spirit.

Faith That Receives Now

It has already been pointed out that faith to be perfect must reach the place where it not only believes that God will, but that He does, right now, what we ask Him to do. Most people who touch bottom in consecration will have little difficulty at this point. Faith will seem to spring up spontaneously out of this glad consciousness of having met conditions. In fact, some will burst through and declare their assurance with no conscious exercise of faith at all. But the faith is there. At other times God requires the seeker to step out on the promises found in the Bible and claim the blessing by sheer determination. Such persons need a very clear understanding of the nature of faith.

When faith "doesn't work." Let us review briefly the nature of faith. It is in God, not in feelings. We do not believe because we feel; we feel because we believe. Faith dependent on feelings will forever be weak and unstable. Faith dependent on a great outpouring of power and ecstasy can be easily attacked by the devil the next day after feelings have subsided. But faith planted solidly on the integrity of God and His Word will be shock-resistant and "sagproof."

We may be sure that genuine faith growing out of true consecration and commitment of self and deep confidence in God does release the cleansing power of the Holy Spirit. Faith *is* effectual. The faith method *does* work. *What about the cases then when it seems to fail?* Many seekers are frightened to make a profession or "take it by faith" because of a previous failure. They once professed but there was no subsequent peace or assurance, and no subsequent inward change.

Consider again the analogy of the light switch. If a man turns a switch and gets no light, there is one thing he will not do, if he is normally intelligent and even moderately acquainted with electrical matters. He won't repudiate the "switch method" of getting light. He won't start sputtering that he never did have faith in this thing anyway. He won't say, "See! Just as I thought—nothing to it!" And the next time his wife says, "Dear, please turn the light switch on," he won't start protesting in a hurt tone of voice, "Never again! I flipped that switch once and it didn't work. Next time I've got to see the light first—then I'll flip the switch."

No, an intelligent man who still found himself in darkness after flipping the switch would not panic, but simply conclude that something was defective in the system, and would proceed to investigate. He would check the light bulb, then the fuse, then look for a broken wire or loose connection. Each time he made a repair he would go back and patiently turn the switch. Even if he had to call in a specialist for help, he would not lose heart. He would persist until he obtained light.

Can we not be as sensible about spiritual things? If the attempt to believe seems strained and abortive and brings no blessing, let us patiently reexamine our consecration. Are we all on the altar? Are we trying to bypass some issue? Are we turning a deaf ear to the gentle voice of the Holy Spirit? Our act of faith will make connections if we are entirely honest and surrendered.

When faith must commit. Two very important cautions are necessary here. Sometimes the conscious awareness of the Spirit's presence is briefly delayed. The Spirit's operation cannot be commanded mechanically, so that the flooding of light is instantaneous in all instances. One pastor told a seeker, "Go home and act as if you were expecting company." The "Company" came —but to *abide*, not just visit. If faith does not bring immediate blessing, yet we have examined and reexamined our consecration and believe it is complete, then there is only one thing to do: Hold steady.

The other caution may be even more vital. No matter how sincere or thorough we are in our attempt to "die out," there will always remain that lurking objection, deep down, until destroyed by the Holy Spirit himself. Some people have never dared to exercise faith because they have never gotten through struggling with that inner objector. They thought they had to quiet every contrary voice in their souls before they could believe. This is a radical error, for it constitutes an attempt to sanctify ourselves. Ours is to say yes even when there is something in us that doesn't want to say yes. Ours is to be willing to be made willing. Ours is to face honestly every issue raised by either the devil, the Holy Spirit, or the carnal mind within us. Ours then is to confess this lurking rebellion to God, deliberately renounce it, ask God to burn it out, then commit it to God. This commitment of our sinful hearts to God to do what we can't do, and what even our consecration can't do, is part of faith itself. We must take the step of faith even when we are conscious that there is a pocket of resistance in our City of Mansoul. For faith is directed specifically to that very pocket of resistance. The divine, supernatural elimination of that resistance is the very thing we are believing for.

This too underscores the necessity of holding steady in our act and attitude of faith. And as we believe, God does work in our inner being—call it subconscious if you like. We may be sure of this. Sooner or later the sweet awareness of this cleansing will surge into our souls. But whether it surges in or seeps in is of little consequence. It is only important to know that the inner peace is there.

Summary

1. Christian faith is essentially complete confidence in the presence, power, wisdom, and integrity of a personal God, who has revealed himself in Christ, and speaks to us in the Bible. It is an affirmation of the heart that God is trustworthy, and that what He says in His Word is true. By thus planting one foot on God's Word as we have it in the Bible, and the other on God's love as seen in Christ, it is able to rise above the limitations of time and sense and lay hold of spiritual realities.

2. God has ordained that the exercise of faith should be the one indispensable condition which the

sinner must meet if he would know experientially the benefits of personal salvation. God can provide, promise, and woo, but man must choose to believe. Though his ability to believe is a gift of grace, imparted by the Spirit, the choice to believe must be his own. To disbelieve God is to deny Him; to deny Him is to forfeit Him. To believe God is to unstop the channel of blessing.

3. We are not only justified by faith, but wholly sanctified by faith as well. The same divine energy of the Spirit necessary to our regeneration must work within us that further change called sanctification. But the measure of His freedom to accomplish this change is determined by the measure of our faith for this specific change. If we believe He cannot purify us from all sin, then He cannot. If we believe He can, we are brought into touch. When we believe that he *does,* He is released within, and the "love of God" is poured into our hearts.

4. But faith has its own "works," not of merit, but of obedience. Without perfect surrender and intelligent, deliberate consecration full faith is impossible. When faith seems paralyzed we must search until we find the cause. And the lurking reluctance we must surrender up for cleansing, believing that God can and will purge it. Finally, what we truly believe we will willingly confess.

For Your Discussion

1. What did the father mean by his cry, "Lord, I believe; help thou mine unbelief" (Mark 9:24)? How does this apply to the seeker after holiness?

2. What is meant by the expression, "Let go and let God"? Is it possible to "let go" in the sense of *giving up* without being satisfied? To "let go" before we have "taken hold" in prayer and heart searching?

3. What is the biblical origin of the saying: "The altar sanctifies the gift"? What is implied by it when used in dealing with seekers? Is this a valid and safe application of the scripture?

4. What are some legitimate promises in the Bible which the seeker may lay hold of for immediate sanctification?

5. Is there a difference between the peace the Holy Spirit gives a seeker and the "peace" of apathy—of lost interest? How can one differentiate?

CHAPTER SEVEN

A Life of Power

Scriptures for background:

Luke 24:45-53; John 15:1-8; 16:7-15; Acts 1:4-8; 4:23-37; Eph. 3:14-21; II Cor. 12:7-10

The line of the old hymn which reads, "Judge not the Lord by feeble sense," was twisted by some discerning wag to "Judge not the Lord by feeble saints." Too many "saints" are feeble, and feeble saints do not glorify God. But there need be none. Abundant provision has been made for a life of power. Every Christian can and should be an example of divine grace, a wonder to angels and demons, an amazement to watching men. And the more feeble a Christian is in *himself*, the more pronounced his power should be, for God said to Paul, "My strength is made perfect in weakness" (II Cor. 12:9). Saints have glowed and radiated and blessed from prisons, from broken homes, in poverty and sorrow, from beds of pain.

"At midnight Paul and Silas prayed, and sang praises unto God." It may have taken them until midnight to cast over on the Lord their temptation to discouragement and depression. At any rate, by midnight depression gave way to prayer, and prayer became song. That was victory, even if there had been no earthquake or converted jailer. The spiritual power that was in them prevailed.

But this is not a "package" of power given to *us*. It is a resource of power in the Holy Spirit, who is given to us. He is the Comforter.

The Fullness of the Spirit

The idea of being filled with the Spirit is difficult to state precisely. The Spirit is a Person—the Third Person of the Trinity—and this fact only deepens the mystery, for we cannot understand how one personality can possess another personality. But the Bible is clear that human persons may be possessed by demons who take control of them. Some glimmering of the invasion of one personality by another is seen in hypnosis. This is psychic control of one human being by another. Since this is possible, we ought not to balk at the concept of Spirit-fullness, even if we cannot altogether explain it.[1]

That Spirit-fullness is not only possible but the *expected norm* for all Christians is made abundantly clear in the Bible. This is predicted in the Old Testament as a universal privilege of the gospel age (Joel 2:28-29), and in the New Testament it is a term descriptive of all whom Jesus baptized with the Spirit. On the Day of Pentecost, and in what is sometimes called the "second Pentecost," they were all "filled with the Holy Spirit" (Acts 2:4; 4:31). Saul, converted on the way to Damascus, was three days later filled with the Spirit (Acts 9:

---

[1]Spirit-fullness is not spiritual hypnosis, however. One is never more aware, alert, and more firmly in control than when Spirit-filled.

17). When the Early Church needed a board of stewards (deacons) to take over the practical task of distributing supplies to the poor widows, we would have supposed that believers who were smart businessmen and knew how to win their way with the old ladies would have been sought. Instead, the apostles insisted that they must have not only practical ability ("wisdom") and be well respected ("of honest report") but that they be "full of the Holy Ghost" (Acts 6:3). It was this fullness which later swung two of them (Stephen and Philip) out into rugged and powerful evangelism. That *all* Christians are expected to experience the Spirit in this measure is made clear by Paul's admonition to the Christians in the pagan city of Ephesus, far from Jerusalem. He exhorted them to "be filled with the Spirit" (Eph. 5:18).[2]

What does it mean then to be filled with the Spirit? It means a complete penetration of the Spirit into the whole man, followed by a complete and continuing control of the whole man. The man thus becomes spiritually-minded. He becomes God-conscious and God-possessed. Because he is "strengthened with might by his Spirit in the inner man," Christ does indeed dwell in his heart by faith, and he does become "rooted and grounded in love" (Eph. 3:16-17). Here truly is the establishing grace!

The idea of fullness suggests:

1. The *inwardness of the Spirit's presence.* Jesus promised, "He dwelleth with you, and shall be in you" (John 14:17). We have not only opened the door, we have flung it wide. We know He has come. We sense His sweet abiding presence. Here is intimacy, communion, reality.

---

[2]The Greek here does not mean to be filled once for all and that is the end of it. Nor does it mean to be forever *becoming* filled, but rather, to remain continuously filled. In other words, live the Spirit-filled life.

He does not need to prove His presence by some special kind of feeling, gift, or miracle, any more than my guest's luggage is a necessary proof of his presence in my home. His own personal presence is self-evident. The Spirit speaks to my spirit.

In this intimacy and inwardness is the indescribable *comforting* power of the Paraclete (John 14:16). Actually the word means "one called alongside to help," but in this case He is One called *inside* to help. "Closer than hands or feet," He can swiftly play upon our moods with praise or burden, recall that scripture at the right moment, give us the right word in reply to our Lord's gainsayers, and greatly warm our hearts with a sense of confidence and security in the hours of turbulence and distress, as a mother comforts her child who is frightened in the darkness. *This comfort is power.* Only the Christian who is himself thus comforted can comfort others.[3]

It is this *inwardness* of the Spirit's ministry which is the key to mental *illumination* as we study the Word, and the key to the sharp *intensification* of our love of the Word. It is also the key to *vitality* and reality in our prayer life. The Spirit helps our infirmities, Paul says, and especially is this aid given in prayer. When prayerfulness too deep for words grips us, we may rejoice, for the Spirit is using us as a channel of intercession. Such praying will not be misdirected by carnal selfishness, for it is the Spirit praying (Rom. 8:26). He prays always in harmony with the will of the Father.

2. Furthermore, the idea of fullness suggests the *totality of the Spirit's possession.* On the Day of Pente-

---

[3] The word "Paraclete" (from *parakaleo*), which is translated *Comforter* in the King James Version, is translated *Counselor* in the RSV, *Advocate* in NEB, and *Helper* in Moffatt. *The Amplified New Testament* also adds *Intercessor, Strengthener,* and *Standby*. Put them together and you have the truth better than any one word can express it alone. The Holy Spirit is all of this and more!

cost the sound as of a rushing mighty wind "filled all the house where they were sitting" (Acts 2:2). No space or place was missed. We do not know the architecture, whether the house was one story, two, or three, whether it had one room or many; but whatever it was, the sound filled them all. So must the Holy Spirit possess us: in the *upstairs* of our nature, our reason, imagination, goals, and aspirations; and in the *basement* of our nature, our appetites and bodily instincts. (Note that there is nothing wrong with the "basement"; a basement is not sinful!) He must also possess the *ground level* of our lives, our affections and associations and activities. This is the level of life where others go in and out, where eyes meet and ears listen and tongues speak. Does the Spirit possess the whole?

When a ministerial group, many years ago, was debating whether to ask Dwight L. Moody to come for a campaign, a jealous preacher is reported to have asked, "Does Mr. Moody have a monopoly on the Holy Ghost?" Another minister replied quietly, "No, but the Holy Ghost has a monopoly on Mr. Moody."

3. Again, there is suggested the *overflow of the Spirit's power*. Fullness means overflow—when the vessel is shaken. When squeezed, a sponge will exude only that which fills it. Spirit-filled Christians have a dynamic, moving quality about their lives. They are not only inwardly fortified against the pressures of the world, but they are outwardly forceful. This does not mean that they have forceful, magnetic personalities. Instead they may be shy and reserved by nature, and *continue* to be. But this means that instead of the world getting at them, they in some quiet, mysterious manner get at the world.

There is a drive in them for God and souls. There is a zest for God's work that doesn't have to be primed by contests and rewards. If they find themselves living where there is no spiritual church, instead of backsliding, they will start a prayer meeting or a Sunday school. If they work in a shop or an office for a year, that shop or office will never be the same again. Not that they stand on a desk and preach a sermon every day—but because they are prayed up, blessed up, and filled up, and have the courage to speak up as the Spirit prompts. But their spiritual "radioactivity" is not simply in saying this or that, but in the indefinable anointing of the Holy Spirit upon their lives which makes their subconscious influence Godward. We all know preachers need the anointing upon their sermons. We must not forget that every Christian needs it upon him *as a person*.

When a man is full of wine, people will know it. Similarly a man filled with the Spirit can be spotted. On the Day of Pentecost the railers said, "These men are full of new wine." And when Paul told the Ephesians to be Spirit-filled, he used this contrast to wine-fullness. Notice Phillips' way of putting it: "Don't get your stimulus from wine . . . but let the Spirit stimulate your souls." Anyone thus excited about life in the Spirit, who is aglow with its romance and adventure, will not hanker as did the Israelites for the leeks and garlic of Egypt. He will not be dolorous and long-faced. The world will say, "That man has something, and it has him. Whatever it is, he is enjoying it, and it seems to be doing him good."

The Gifts of the Spirit

The Holy Spirit is himself the great *Gift* to the Church and to the believer. He is the One whom we should seek, and whom we must honor daily. He, in turn, will stir us, prompt us, guide and teach us, check, and if need be, rebuke us. He desires to supervise our lives at every point where He sees there is an issue (no matter how small) which is relevant to either our holiness or our usefulness. In all of this He will be revealing Christ *to* us, forming Christ *in* us, and presenting Christ *through* us. By our lives as well as by our words He will constantly be convicting the world about us "of sin, and of righteousness, and of judgment" (John 16:8). We don't need to be anxious about the matter; He will work through us whether we know it or not. Every holy person is himself redemptive. Every Spirit-filled believer is a channel of power.

But in addition to His personal ministry in us and through us, there are special abilities which the Holy Spirit gives to Christians to meet special demands in His service. These *gifts* may be given, upon occasion, even to immature, unsanctified Christians—though lurking selfishness within may trip them into gloating over the gift rather than glorying in the Giver.

Nine of these gifts Paul lists in I Cor. 12:8-10. In this chapter also he discusses the underlying principles. They can be stated as follows:

1. No apparent gift has its source in the Holy Spirit unless it glorifies Jesus as Lord (v. 3).

2. The purpose of the gifts is the profiting or edification of the Church and the conviction and conversion of sinners (v. 7b; also 2:3-5).

3. The distribution of the gifts is entirely the Spirit's business, not ours (v. 11). We exercise the gifts given, but we do not specify which shall be given. We are His servants, not His managers.

Living Letters paraphrases Paul's list this way:

> To one person the Spirit gives the ability to give wise advice; someone else may be especially good at studying, and this is his gift from the same Spirit. He gives special faith to another, and to someone else the power to cure the sick. He gives power for doing miracles to some; and power to prophesy and preach to others. He gives someone else the power to know whether evil spirits are speaking through those who claim to be giving God's messages—or whether it is really the Spirit of God Who is speaking. Still another person is able to speak in languages he never

learned; and others, who do not know the language either, are given power to understand what he is saying.[4]

These gifts can be traced unmistakably through The Acts:

1. *Wisdom* is seen in James as he handles the divided first General Assembly and pronounces a decision for the entire Church (Acts 15).

2. *Knowledge* is exemplified in Luke, the author who, as an inspired scholar, gathered the facts and wrote the history. Was he not given special ability to write accurately and with balanced perspective?

3. *Faith* was given to Ananias, who first drew back in panic from going to Saul but in the end was enabled to walk boldly into the house with the greeting, "Brother Saul..." (Acts 9:10-17).

4. Gifts of *healing* are seen in Peter and John (3:1-8) and others.

5. The *working of miracles* is seen in Peter raising Dorcas (9:39) and found also in the deacon Stephen (6:8) and in Paul (13:11).

6. *Prophecy*, in the sense of *forthtelling*, is seen in Peter's masterful, inspired sermon on the Day of Pentecost (2:14 f.), and, in the sense of *foretelling*, in Paul (20:23, 29; 27:22-26) and Agabus (Acts 11:28).

7. *Discernment of spirits* is manifest in Peter dealing with Ananias and Sapphira (5:1-11) and with Simon the sorcerer (8:23).

8. *Kinds of tongues* were given on the Day of Pentecost to the 120 (2:4), to the household of Cornelius (10:46), and to the disciples at Ephesus (19:6). There seems to be no specific instance in The Acts of the *interpretaion of tongues.*

[4]Kenneth N. Taylor, *Living Letters* (Tyndale House, Publishers, 1962).

It is probably better to think of these gifts as occasional enduements to meet emergencies, not necessarily permanent endowments. Peter may not always have been able to "see through" people as he did Ananias and Sapphira. Paul was not always able to exercise the gifts of healing (II Tim. 4:20).

Furthermore, the gifts are not always spectacular or sensational. The best gifts, wisdom and knowledge, needed so desperately by the administrator and teacher, are not very exciting. Certainly they are not self-advertised.

No doubt this is one phase of power promised by Jesus (Acts 1:8) which should abide in the Church in all ages. We can expect God to do the unusual. We can expect Him to use us in special ways. Normally this power will supplement and augment one's natural abilities, bringing out hidden potential no one suspected. But at times these manifestations of power, when *really needed*, and *strictly at the Spirit's* discretion, will be beyond human explanation. Actually in every spiritual church there is more of this than we sometimes recognize. It is proper to pray for larger manifestations of the Spirit, and to "covet earnestly the best gifts," especially the gift of *prophecy* (14:1). If anyone is tempted to believe that this valuable gift is scarce, he should visit a few lively, typical holiness churches on Wednesday nights!

The Graces of the Spirit

It is a mistake to assume that when one has been filled with the Spirit he will immediately be a powerful preacher and an effective revivalist. Reading the life of Charles G. Finney, one young man thrilled to the vivid accounts of mighty movings, and leaped to the conclusion that such power was the norm for all. The natural logic of his position was that he did not have the promised "power" (Acts 1:8) of the fullness of the Spirit, unless sinners fell under pungent conviction and revivals broke out everywhere he went. So he prayed and waited for this power for years, but in vain. In the meanwhile he was a carping, cynical, useless Christian, unable even to get along with his wife. The truth might have dawned on him had he read with seeing eyes Acts 4:33: "And with great power gave the apostles witness of the resurrection of the Lord Jesus: and great grace was upon them all."

Only the apostles, and to a lesser extent the deacons and other functionaries (cf. Eph. 4:11), were anointed with special concentrated power for a public ministry. But there was another kind of power, just as divine, and even more vital, which all shared: the power of "great grace." This was the main line of power even for the apostles, for miracle-working and preaching power had been given them *before* Pentecost (Matt. 10:1, 7-8). The power of Pentecost purified their motives and made them *saints* in the richest sense of that word. It cemented them in bonds of love, stabilized them with unshakable assurance, and fired them with unquenchable zeal and heroism and sacrifice. This was a deeper, more basic, more indispensable power than the other. This made *witnesses* out of them, not only in what they said and in what they did, but in what they *were*. And this kind of power, available to all, both then and now, is the *real hallmark of Spirit-fullness*.

It is impossible to exaggerate the importance of this power. In comparison to it gifts are very secondary. Life is rough on us. We will be buffeted, oppressed, slandered, and we must have *grace* to face it. Enough grace, in fact, to *live* the Sermon on the Mount, to love our enemies, and pray without rancor for those who despitefully use us! We must have enough to demonstrate before doctors and employers and loved ones that God "hath not given us the spirit of fear; but of power, and of love, and of a sound mind" (written by Paul in prison—II Tim. 1:7). If the Holy Spirit reigns, this kind of power will be increasingly manifest.

The fundamental grace of the Spirit is love, which He pours into our hearts abundantly (Rom. 5:5). Love is the key to Christlikeness, and *Christlikeness is power.* Love is the secret also of poise as we face death and the judgment, for "perfect love casteth out fear" (I John 4:17-18). *Poise is power.*

When we have been sanctified wholly, and the love of God has been "shed abroad" in our hearts, the Holy Spirit at once nurtures and develops all of the associated graces. In Gal. 5:22 these graces are called "fruit." They are, in addition to love: "joy, peace, longsuffering, gentleness, goodness, faith, meekness, temperance." Love is the "bond of perfectness" (Col. 3:14), the cement which holds the various graces together and "completes the whole" (NEB). We can well think of the nine graces or fruits as *aspects* of love. If so—

Joy is the *glow* of love.

Peace is the *harmony* (within) and *peaceableness* (without) of love.

Long-suffering is the *patience* of love—its refusal to fight back.

Gentleness is the *kindness* of love—its courtesy, even when dealing faithfully with the erring.

Goodness is the *benevolence* of love—its generosity and magnanimity.

Faith is the *faithfulness* of love—its dependability and steadfastness.

Meekness is the *humility* and submissiveness of love—the meek man is not "heady and highminded," determined to "rule or ruin."

Temperance is the *self-control*, the discipline of love. The Spirit-filled person, impelled by love, is not living for self.

Love is more concerned about making others happy than simply being happy. Here is the free man, and *freedom is power*. Such a man lives in conformity to law, yet free from law, for he has crucified the flesh with its affections and lusts. Against the fruit of the Spirit "there is no law." His is not the bondage of the carnal man, enslaved by his lusts, nor the bondage of the legalist, enslaved by his fears. His is rather the bondage of love in delightful servitude to Christ. Pity him not, for his is the bondage that is perfect freedom.

The fruit of the Spirit begins to grow when we are born again, but it is often mixed with the works of the flesh. This does not mean the grosser sins from which we are saved in conversion, but the emotional manifestations of unsanctified human nature which continue to disturb. Among these are "hatred [grudges], variance [quarreling], emulations [keeping up with the Joneses], wrath [fits of temper, strife, rivalry], seditions [whispering campaigns, disloyalty], heresies [party spirit], envyings [unhappiness over the prosperity and happiness of others]." These are "sour grapes" that pucker the mouth. Many times a Christian's influence is spoiled by the outcropping of a carnal trait.

But the Spirit-filled Christian is characterized consistently by freedom from the works of the flesh and a *growing* manifestation of the Spirit. It works something like this: the fruit, by His regenerating and sanctifying power, becomes impregnated into our total character, so that we can say this is what we *are*. Then increasingly these graces which are within work their way out through our personalities, our voices, manner, actions, and reactions, and thus we are changed into the image of Christ "from glory to glory" (II Cor. 3:18).

When once love has been enthroned, the "firstfruits" of joy and peace come easily. These are precious and indispensable. Then come long-suffering, gentleness, goodness, faith. The slowest to mature are meekness and temperance, not because we are unsanctified, but because we are sometimes slow to see that rigorous discipline in the area of the *natural,* and submissiveness in the realm of human relationships, belong to holiness. We are too dull to see easily the difference between courage in standing for convictions and bullheadedness in fighting for opinions. Or possibly the real slowness is learning how to tell a legitimate, Bible-based conviction from a secondhand, emotion-based opinion.

By nature, also, some are more independent than others. When delivered from love of men's applause and fear of men's opinions they swing to the other extreme. The Spirit must teach them that too much independence is as bad as too little. We should be independent of the world, but *submissive* to our brethren. But these graces will ripen too, given a little time. The Spirit will see to that, even if in the process the heart must be broken in order to crack a thick head. But the *power*—by which is meant the spiritual impact—increases as the graces of the Spirit grow.

The Purpose of Power

Why do we desire power? To enjoy it? Display it? Exploit it? Then we will not receive it.

It is said that in 1927 when the king of England broadcast his annual Christmas message, and arrangements were made for it to be picked up in New York and transmitted to America, a careless workman tripped over a vital wire and broke it. There not being time to repair it, a technician grasped the two severed ends, one in each hand, and conveyed the message through his body.[5] We may be sure he did not run that risk simply to feel power, but to *transmit* power; more than that, to transmit a *message,* even the message of the king! When we are totally consumed by the passion to transmit the mes-

---

[5] I have not been able to verify the historical accuracy of this. However, two transmitting technicians have told me that under some circumstances such a thing is possible.

sage of *our* King, we will be where God can trust us with power.

But it will not always be a *conscious* power. We will at times, in our efforts to witness or preach, *feel* feeble and defeated, only to discover later that virtue flowed from the Spirit through us to bless needy hearts. I once heard L. A. Reed preach in a camp meeting, when I could sense the deep moving of the Spirit in the area where I sat. I felt that God was at work, especially upon the unsaved man next to me who had consented to come to his first religious service in many years. Suddenly the preacher stopped and pleaded, "Saints, pray! Satan is fighting, and I'm having a hard time." Power was flowing through him, but he was not aware of it.

Feeling power therefore is unimportant; the surrender to the Spirit as His instrument is all-important. His purpose is not that we will be glorified. It does not matter how much or how little the Spirit witnesses to us, as long as we are enabled to bear witness unto Christ.

No one can say whether, in witnessing, word or life is more urgent. Neither is dispensable. The redeemed of the Lord must say so in public testimony before the congregation and in private testimony to the neighbor and the friend. But backing up the testimony must be a consistently holy life and a merciful, warm, loving spirit. "Ye shall be witnesses unto me" not only as oral advertisers but living samples. This is both the purpose and the fulfillment of the promised power (Acts 1:8).

Summary

We have been thinking together about the solemn responsibility upon professedly Spirit-filled Christians to prove their blessing by living lives of power.

Let us remind ourselves that this promised and available power is *not*—

1. A "package" of power that we can store within and use at will, without continued prayer, obedience,

and constant dependence on the Holy Spirit as our Power-Source.

2. A "conscious" power which we can always recognize within ourselves to our own satisfaction.

3. A "pulpit" power which will make great speakers and revivalists out of all.

4. A "success" power which will guarantee health, wealth, and prosperity, and project us into places of leadership.

5. An "immunity" power by which we can infallibly ward off all misfortunes, calamities, and sorrows.

Positively, it *is*—

1. The power of *sheer goodness*. Holiness is the foundation of all spiritual power. "My strength is as the strength of ten because my heart is pure," testified the poet. Sometimes the remark is made: "He is good, but good for nothing." Impossible! True goodness, which reminds men of Jesus, is inherently forceful. There is no power mightier than the power of character.

2. The power of *overflowing love* that reaches up for more of God and reaches out for lost souls. Such love rises above the shabby and petty to be redemptive.

3. The power of *special grace* for special needs, and of special enablings for divinely appointed tasks. We can say with Paul: "God is able to make all grace abound toward you; that ye, always having all sufficiency in all things, may abound to every good work" (II Cor. 9:8), and, "I can do all things through Christ which strengtheneth me" (Phil. 4:13).

QUESTIONS FOR DISCUSSION

1. Several short propositions are scattered throughout this chapter ending with ". . . is power." What are they? Do you agree?

2. In what way is the power of holy character mightier than the power of spectacular gifts?

3. What are the dangers in becoming obsessively concerned about "gifts"?

4. Is it possible for a Christian to be truly sanctified wholly, yet not be living "in the Spirit" to the degree which is his privilege? If so, what are the perils of such living?

5. Does a Christian possess his maximum degree of spiritual power when he is baptized with the Spirit, or should we expect an increase of power over the years?

6. What can be said about Christians who have professed for five, ten, or more years to be "Spirit-filled" yet are noticeably lacking in the fruit of the Spirit, with no sign of improvement?

CHAPTER EIGHT

The Guidance of the Spirit

Scriptures for background:

Genesis 27; Psalms 32; Acts 8: 5-40; 16: 1-13; Col. 3: 12-20; Eph. 5: 6-17; I Tim. 6: 1-11.

The privilege of divine guidance is a dimension to the Christian life which is little understood and perhaps even less enjoyed. The wild claims of fanatics have made some people shy about claiming any guidance in their lives at all. Others have hesitated to explore this mysterious spiritual world because to them it smacked of magic. Still others have been slow to believe that God is sufficiently interested in them to take them by the hand as a father leads a child. But Christians who hang back are missing blessing, security, and usefulness.

Abraham's servant was able to rejoice in the success of his mission to obtain a wife for his master's son, Isaac, because he was able to say, "I being in the way, the Lord led me to the house of my master's brethren" (Gen. 24: 27).

The Lord led me! What a high adventure! One thing is sure: the child of God who seriously sets about the business of learning the art of divine guidance, and desires that each day he shall know something of the direct leading of the Spirit, will never lack for romance and excitement in the Christian way. There will be in his heart a never-ending sense of the reality of the supernatural, of the nearness and sweetness of the divine.

More important than personal enrichment, however, will be the multiplied usefulness of the one life which God has given to invest. When the Holy Spirit leads, there is accomplished what the Holy Spirit designs; when He does not lead, there are frustration and failure. It cannot be otherwise. If we had several lives with which to experiment, we could afford to grope our way in strange paths and bungle unfamiliar opportunities, because the errors which we made the first time could be avoided the next time. But we pass this way but once, and if we miss the path of God's will we will have missed it forever. Therefore it is not only man's greatest privilege to be able to find God's will for life's crossroads, but it is his supreme duty.

Areas of Guidance

In righteous living. Since we read in the Scriptures that they who are led by the Spirit of God are the sons of God, we must begin here, and remind ourselves that in a general sense all Christians are being led every day whether they fully realize it or not. The Holy Spirit is prompting them toward spiritual things and toward heaven as their ultimate goal. They are as Christian in *Pilgrim's Progress*. In spite of their blundering and staggering, the Lord always has some means of guidance here and there at critical junctures in their path.

In detecting heresy. To a great extent even the perception of true and false doctrine which children of God have is astonishing. They need instructors, true;

but the Holy Spirit will give them a remarkable sensitivity to false prophets and doctrinal error. James C. Lentz of the World Gospel Mission tells of a customs officer in Mexico who was remarkably converted, but who had to be left on his own by the missionary with nothing but the Scriptures and the Holy Spirit to guide him. Thirteen months later when the missionary returned he found the man, though holding steady, was a bit puzzled. Pointing to thirteen attractively bound religious books which he had eagerly purchased from a passing colporteur, he said: "I started to read, but something in here [pointing to his heart] said to me, 'Don't read these books!' " They were Jehovah's Witness books. Though he had never heard of the cult, the Holy Spirit protected him.

In witnessing. Jesus said to the disciples, "Follow me, and I will make you fishers of men." It is through the ministry of the Holy Spirit that our Lord continues to carry on the training of His disciples. It is well to study manuals and methods in personal evangelism and other forms of Christian work, but in the end it is the Spirit alone who knows infallibly when it is time to speak and when it is time to be silent. Glib, bubbling talkers do not always make the best soul winners. Even fervent public testimonies at times can be in the energy of the flesh and for the glory of self, rather than in the Spirit and for the glory of God. It is not so much the human tact, approach, or eloquence which makes either a personal word or a public sermon powerful as it is the amount of God there is in it. One layman became exercised in spirit over the profanity used by his supervisor when haranguing the employees in their occasional meetings. The layman prayed much for divine guidance and then when the Holy Spirit prompted him, and providentially gave him the opportunity, he responded. Although dozens of men were standing around, he stood up to the supervisor and rebuked him—but he did so with tears running down his cheeks. The supervisor dropped his head for a moment, then said quietly, "Thank you." There was no profanity at the next meeting. But to have attempted such a confrontation without the guidance and the tenderness of the Spirit would have done more harm than good.

Occasionally silence is more eloquent than words. As an old Scotsman said once to Oswald Chambers, "If you do not understand the sealing of the lips in silence, you do not understand the work of the Holy Spirit."

In practical matters. Every day will be brighter if at its beginning we can confidently and boldly ask for the guidance of the Spirit in our practical, even minor, daily concerns. People have been shown where to find lost articles. Doctors have been given special guidance and aid in delicate operations. A midwest farmer was about to buy a piece of property, thinking it was a rare bargain, but obeyed the check of the Holy Spirit and refrained. His guidance was vindicated later on when the winds of the dust bowl denuded that particular property to a barren wasteland. Who can experience the thrill of seeing the hand of God obviously work in one's life—in the open or closed door, in the dramatic protection, in the distinct sense of leadership soon justified by events—and *ever doubt that God cares?*

In life's vocation. God has plans, not just for preachers and missionaries, but for all of His children. The consecrated, Spirit-filled young man who becomes a farmer should not do so simply because he has not been called to anything else and knows nothing else to do. He, as well as anyone, has a right to pray for and expect a sense of leadership in his life. He needs a sense of *vocation,* so that if he becomes a farmer it is with a deep conviction that farming is exactly what God wants him to do. This will add dignity to his life, galvanize his activities with a concept of mission, and sanctify his enjoyment of the soil.

In life's partnerships. We must choose not only vocation and location but also the people with whom we live and with whom we work. Why shouldn't businessmen pray about the associations they form in business? God knows the secrets of human character better than our poor judgment can ferret them out. God the Holy Spirit can warn us of the scoundrel and confidence man.

But the most solemn partnership is that entered into when a man and woman stand before the sacred altar and vow lifelong fidelity to each other. That partner will either help or hinder our getting to heaven. Prayer for guidance in this crucial choice of life should begin at a very young age, unashamedly. God is interested in helping a young person achieve domestic happiness and enrichment, and has a plan which He can work out in his own way and time. If the young person is convinced of this, he will be less apt, impatiently and prematurely, to enter into rash and unwise relationships. The time to pray is *before* couples fall in love rather than afterward. At the infatuation stage our minds play tricks on us, so that we tend to secure the answer that we humanly desire. But if we have prayed enough *before* falling in love, our judgment will be more mature.

QUALIFICATIONS FOR SUCCESSFUL GUIDANCE

But who can qualify for this kind of guidance? At least three qualities are basic:

Pure motives. The underlying master motive of life of course must be to seek the glory of God and do the will of God. There are, however, secondary motives which in their place are legitimate. To talk, then, about pure motives does not mean that self-interest or self-pleasure must never be a consideration in our desire to be led by the Lord. Our own happiness, our own freedom from pain, and the prosperity and success of our undertakings are always important to us. God does not require that this shall be otherwise. When a young man asks the Lord to direct him to the right girl as his life's mate, who would say that his own happiness is not a consideration in this request? By "pure motive" we mean two things: first, that all personal considerations are subordinated always to the master motive, and secondly, that our motives are free from all deceit.

An excellent proof of such purity of motive is the kind of unselfishness demonstrated by Deacon Philip when the apostles from Jerusalem came to Samaria and displaced him as leader of the great revival. Instead of being the center of attention in a big city, he found himself in the desert. When the Holy Spirit gave him directions in the desert, he was just as quick and cheerful in his obedience as when he had been receiving guidance in Samaria. This is the sort of unselfishness which is basic.

Honest willingness. There must be an inner submissiveness to the will of God, so that we are enabled to be willing, in the crisis, *to be led either way.* This is not always easy, for the natural man, even though sanctified, shrinks from some things and prefers others. We prefer to be led in pleasant paths rather than in stony, rugged ways. But in searching for the mind of the Lord in a specific situation we must surrender our preferences, and get to the place in our searching where we are genuinely willing to go either way. The promise is, "The meek will he guide in judgment" (Ps. 25:9). Only the meek are willing to be guided, and only the meek are humble enough to acknowledge their need of guidance. A self-sufficient man, as a willful child running from his mother, is sure that he can find his own way and will not bother to pray about his decisions. But the meek man does not have such boundless confidence in his own judgment. He knows that always there are hidden factors beyond his view which only God comprehends. Therefore, instead of looking to himself he looks to God. He is not weak, but he is tamed. His pride is cleansed and his impetuosity is disciplined. He is willing to ask for and wait for the guidance of God.

Constant prayerfulness. It is only as we keep in touch (and in tune) with God through a spirit of prayer that we have any hope of learning the art of guidance. We must want guidance enough to ask for it daily. In our praying we should ask for the illumination of our minds and for sound judgment. We should pray for sensitivity to the pressure of the Holy Spirit on our spirits, for insight into hindrances in ourselves or others, and for ability to read the signposts of providence. We need to seek for the quickening of the Scripture for our need. All of these are legitimate requests, for each is involved in obtaining guidance. We can wisely pray also for patience to wait for clarity and for grace to be obedient. If we sincerely ask, God will save us from being deceived either by the false "light" of Satan or by the imagination of our own minds.

Although *conscious* guidance about recognized problems is what we have chiefly in mind, it is well to pray for unconscious guidance too. This is that steering of our lives, that ordering of our steps (and *stops*), when we are preoccupied with other things. Then, also, we certainly will ask God to overrule our mistakes. Though prayerfulness and a spirit of obedience will reduce both the number and seriousness of our errors, we will still make some. We must not suppose that the Holy Spirit makes us infallible.

But in the many things which puzzle us, and which may be more significant than we know, we can lift our hearts to the Lord for the gentle touch of His Spirit on ours. After all, the promise of the Word is that He will guide us with His eye. Some of us who are married know what that means. At first when we are newly married it is difficult to communicate, and difficult to interpret the other's awkward attempts to get a message to us. The frustrated spouse may have to resort to gentle kicks under the table or to other highly unsatisfactory means, but the time comes when a raised eyebrow is enough. In fact, people who are still in love and have lived together for many years can almost anticipate one another's thoughts. This is the way Enoch walked with God, and it is the way we may walk with God—if we walk with Him long enough and close enough.

It is a great mistake for us to feel that God in His almightiness is above paying attention to the little things in our lives, as if they were too trifling. God is not indifferent to anything that is of vital concern to His child. As one "mother in Israel" used to say: "If it is big enough to talk about, it is big enough to pray about." We do not honor God by our reluctance to confide in Him concerning the common things which disturb us. Rather we limit Him, and rob ourselves of blessings which He would be pleased to bestow. This is not self-centeredness; it is the father-child relationship into which God has been pleased to enter with us.

This constant prayerfulness in our quest for guidance will gradually develop in us a keen sensitivity to spiritual issues and realities. It will teach us to "walk circumspectly, not as fools, but as wise" (Eph. 5:15). When we cultivate this frame of mind, it will be easier for the Holy Spirit to get our attention. He will be able to break through the barrier of our busyness, and impress on our minds His check or prompting.

How the Holy Spirit Guides

When Philip was sent down to the desert, not knowing why, he probably sat by the roadside, pondering the strange turn of events. As he glanced up he saw this glittering chariot approaching, carrying an Ethiopian V.I.P. Philip may have felt just a little awed. Suddenly the "Spirit said unto Philip, Go near, and join thyself to this chariot" (Acts 8:29).

Some time later, in Antioch, the church elders were praying and fasting, when, unexpectedly, "the Holy Ghost said, Separate me Barnabas and Saul for the work whereunto I have called them" (Acts 13:2). In each of these cases the Spirit is said to *speak,* directly, clearly, and unmistakably. How does the Spirit "speak" to us?

By positive impression. It is not likely that either Philip or the group at Antioch heard an audible voice. It was an inward voice. A strong urge took possession of them which they intuitively recognized as the Spirit's prompting. When once experienced, this is never to be forgotten. Many times our impressions will be weak, vague, and cloudy, and we will be filled with uncertainties. But at other times there is a flash of insight that seems to penetrate the mysterious veil of events, and we see clearly what we should do. It may come as a sense of duty, which has now become sharply focused and satisfying. Often this sky-blue conviction, this peaceful assurance of duty, reaches its peak of certainty gradually. It begins as a gentle impression that disturbs the consciousness, robs of sleep, perhaps, and cannot quite be put out of the mind. Then it gradually ripens into a calm, unshakable conviction.

But generally the crisis comes in a time of special prayer, such as at Antioch, or in a crucial moment such as Philip faced with the approaching chariot. In such cases it may be unexpected, and for that reason almost unrecognized. A pastor in an Oklahoma city was driving home one day from an afternoon of calling, when he was suddenly aware of a strong urge to stop at a certain big house on the corner. He knew nothing about the house or its occupants. Not wanting to do anything foolish, and not immediately assured that it was the Spirit's voice prompting him, he drove on. But the impression became more urgent with every passing moment, so he turned back. When the old man who met him at the door learned that he was the local pastor, he burst into tears.

For many years he had been away from God—a backslidden preacher. Over the past three weeks he and his wife had been trying to get back to God. That very morning they had prayed that if there was any hope for them a preacher would be sent to their home that day. Secretly the old man had determined to commit suicide if no one came.

Here is a twentieth-century example that is as authentic as the accounts in The Acts. What if there had not been someone living sufficiently close to God to hear the Spirit's voice and obey!

By a sense of restraint. This we might call a negative impression. It takes the form of a cloud over our spirits, a sense of uneasiness, an awareness of danger prompting us to stop. We feel a restraining hand on our shoulders. Again we can find a perfect example in the Scriptures, this time in Acts 16:6-7. After having gone through Phrygia and Galatia, Paul evidently desired to evangelize in the area more thoroughly. But he and Silas "were forbidden by the Holy Ghost to preach the word in Asia."[1] Traveling on in unaccustomed silence, they reached the district of Mysia. Here the muzzled and puzzled preachers tried to turn northeastward toward Bithynia, "but the Spirit suffered them not." A red light was flashed inside them which they dared not ignore. *Their* judgment and desire pointed to Bithynia, but when they started to move in that direction the heaviness on their spirits deepened. They knew they must not persist in that course. So with growing frustration and bewilderment they moved on west to Troas, on the Aegean Sea. It was there they received the specific "Macedonian call."

---

[1] This was not Asia as we know it today, but the Roman province by this name, of which Phrygia, Mysia, Lydia, and Caria were districts, with Ephesus the provincial capital. It is now western Turkey.

Before we leave this subject of guidance by *shadows* we might profitably examine briefly the three usual reasons for this sort of guidance.

1. Sometimes the restraint is intended as a plain, positive, permanent *denial*. This inviting path, this alluring course of action, is simply not God's will for us, now or ever, so let's forget it. One man tells in his autobiography of praying and fasting three days about a young woman whom he thought would make a suitable preacher's wife. The longer he prayed, the more depressed he felt about the prospect until he finally conceded that God was trying to impress a big, round NO into his thick skull. When years later he learned what a shrew she turned out to be, he exclaimed, "Praise the Lord, I didn't get her!"

2. Again, this sort of guidance may be intended only as a *delay*. While Paul never was permitted to preach in Bithynia, he was permitted later to return to Asia. In Ephesus, in fact, he enjoyed his longest and possibly most successful ministry.

3. Or the guidance by restraint may be a *diversion* of routing or method, in the interest of personal safety or success. A church may be restrained from buying a certain lot for no apparent reason; subsequent developments may disclose God's provision for a better lot, or possibly the same one at a better price.

As far as safety is concerned, numberless Christians have saved their lives by obeying the checks of the Spirit. When World War I broke out, Dr. H. F. Reynolds was in Argentina. He went to the travel agency in Buenos Aires to book his passage home on the only ship scheduled to sail directly to New York. While he was in the process of making the purchase, the Spirit urged, "Better not!" Not at first recognizing the true source of the impression, he proceeded with the arrangements. But when he heard that inner voice the third time saying, "Better not!" he confessed his experience to the ticket agent. The man replied, "If I heard a voice like that, you couldn't hire me to board this ship!" Dr. Reynolds then purchased passage on a ship that would reach New York only after a perilous detour by way of Africa. In the end he safely reached home, while the "safer" ship, which the Spirit forbade him to take, was sunk by the enemy. While it would be unfair and untrue to conclude that every accident or calamity in a Christian's life represents a missed cue somewhere, one cannot help wondering, nevertheless, how many tragedies God has tried to save His children from by flashing red lights that went unheeded. Certainly God could still save His people by other means, and doubtless often does, but there seems to be evidence that at times He chooses not to. The reasons are hidden deep in His own wisdom and sovereignty. On the more positive side, it should be said that a Christian who is spared by obeying such a restraint knows that he has had an experience which makes God more real. It serves to deepen both his sense of dependence and his sense of responsibility.

By rational deduction. We must return to Paul once more. One night while at Troas, praying and waiting for directions, Paul had the famous vision of the man of Macedonia, saying, "Come over into Macedonia, and help us" (Acts 16:9). Now notice the remarkable statement that follows: "And after he had seen the vision, immediately we endeavoured to go into Macedonia, assuredly gathering that the Lord had called us for to preach the gospel unto them." He did not ascribe the call to the "man of Macedonia," but to the Lord. The Lord had been weaving a pattern which now became recognizable. To *assuredly gather* is to put two and two together and make four. This is rational deduction. It is ruminating on several odd-shaped events that seem not to make sense, then suddenly perceiving that if we put them together carefully the jigsaw puzzle will make a clear and obvious picture. Then we can move with confidence. It is in this sort of guidance that God will "guide [the meek] in judgment" (Ps. 25:9).

In the previous instances the form of guidance was the direct and immediate revelation of the Spirit—"the Holy Ghost said." But in this instance there is a combination of experiences before assurance is reached, and one factor is the exercise of our own minds in reading these various signposts and making sense out of them. Restraint—blockade—Troas—and now this *vision;* I therefore *conclude.* The probability is that most experiences of significant, life-altering guidance are of this kind.

But Paul's experience is typical in another respect too. Obtaining clear guidance in the more crucial decisions of life often seems very difficult. We go through a period of deep bewilderment, when we are tempted to wonder if it makes a snap of difference to God what we do. We find ourselves exclaiming: "I wish the Lord would speak right out loud!" At such times young people, in confusion, come to their pastor and ask, "How can we really *know?*" Paul, and thousands of saints since, would sympathize with them. Nevertheless with one voice they would answer: "Make sure you really want guidance, then *hold steady* and God will find a way of letting you know in the nick of time."

Sometimes the delay is part of the divine plan, as when the Lord must get us to our "Troas" before it is "right" to give us the vision. Sometimes, however, the excessive uncertainty and suspense are due rather to our own slowness in seeing the signals our Guide is trying to give us. The process of obtaining guidance will become less painful and prolonged if we learn more skillfully to read God's road map, signs, and cues. Therefore let us examine more minutely the various factors we must always consider if we are to make a "rational deduction" safely, and with valid assurance.

Testing the "Spirits"

There are many "spirits," or winds of doctrine and impression (see Eph. 4:14), which will play upon our consciousness. Some will be purely human, others demonic. At times these spurious impressions will seem genuine divine leadings. Only very careful, prayerful, honest examination will save us from being deceived by them. Let us learn to test impressions by certain touchstones.

The Scriptures. This does not mean that the Bible is to be used as a form of "casting lots" and that when we want guidance all we need to do is shut our eyes, open the Bible at random, drop a finger on a verse, and then proceed to twist it into some kind of interpretation that is relative to our problems. For one thing, this is an evasion of sound thinking. For another, it ignores the basic role of the Spirit in illuminating our minds. Therefore this method can be the most dangerously deceptive of all. It is not what one verse says—or can be twisted to say—that matters; it is rather the light which can be thrown on our problems by the whole Bible. Is our impression consistent with sound doctrine, especially relating to Christ? John insists, for instance, that any cult or prophet which is not straight on both the true deity and true humanity of Jesus Christ is thereby proved false. Any impression favorable to such a movement, or inclining us into it or to support it, is not of God (I John 4:1-2).

How does the Holy Spirit use Scripture to throw light on our way? (1) By quickening to our memories some pertinent passage while we are prayerfully and thoughtfully seeking His will. (2) By illuminating some portion in our regular reading, and flashing it as a torch on our problems; we see in it, not imagined relevance, but real guidance. (3) By helping us as we diligently *search* the Bible for some clear word. This is difficulty for the beginner, who is unacquainted with the Bible's total message and overall tone, and who is not adept in finding his way around in it. The Spirit often gives special help through older Christians in such cases.

The conscience. The greatest help to be found in the Scriptures is the basic guidance it gives in determining what is right. Having determined this, we can then decisively reject all impressions which involve the least compromise with right. We can adopt as a rule of thumb the dictum that the Lord will not lead us to violate our consciences.

One qualification is necessary here, however. At times the Lord may be trying to reeducate the conscience, to bring it more into harmony with the Bible. A certain Christian worker picked up the notion that because oysters did not meet the Levitical standards for "clean" meats it was wrong for her as a Christian to eat them. Therefore she banned them from her diet, though she was very fond of them. Shortly there came a time of extreme financial stringency, even empty cupboards. Since she was pastoring a little church, she prayed, "Lord, impress someone to invite me home for dinner." The prayer was answered, and they all sat down to—an oyster feed! Inwardly she groaned: "Lord, what shall I do?" Gently the Spirit whispered: "Whatsoever is set before you, eat, asking no questions for conscience sake" (I Cor. 10:27). In this way the Spirit reeducated her conscience.

But a reeducation of the conscience, if of the Lord, will always be *toward* sound biblical principles of righteousness, never *away* from them. It isn't the Spirit that would encourage going to places and doing things in the name of broad-mindedness which are incompatible with Bible standards of holy living.

Some people have claimed to be led of the Lord to do things others seriously questioned. Christians have professed guidance about entering into business partnerships with unbelievers. Harried businessmen have felt impressed to get around their financial problems in shady ways. Adulterers and adulteresses have boldly claimed that God blessed them as they "prayed" together. And so we might go on compiling ways sinful hearts have hidden behind professed divine guidance as a shield for their unholy deeds. But anything that is not right according to clear Bible teaching must not be attributed to the Holy Spirit. The Holy Spirit will authorize no one to hew his own moral path, and be a law unto himself.

Providence. We have already spoken of acquiring skill in reading the Lord's signposts. These are the events and circumstances which shape our lives. The faith of the Christian is that, though we have little control over these events, God does. He is perfectly able to arrange a series of outer circumstances which will crowd us into His path, and which at the same time will match the inner guidance of the Spirit. Our impressions should find some confirmation in "ships" waiting in the harbor to transport us from our Troas to our Macedonia. If there are no "ships," if there is nothing but closed doors and empty harbors, we may be sure that either our urge is mistaken or the time is not yet ripe. If the urge persists, as we continue to pray, then we can confidently wait for the revelation of God's timing in the unfolding of events.

But such waiting goes against the grain of activist moderns. Whatever virtues we may have, the ability to wait patiently is not one of them. The general feeling is that a stick of dynamite is a legitimate bit of equipment for our Christian worker's kit—for the purpose of blasting open locked doors! In many ways we take things into our own hands and assume the role of Providence. Sometimes a little initiative is all to the good.

But when delicate questions of the divine will are being decided, this impatient, rough manipulation of circumstances can work untold havoc. By our impetuousness we can foul up God's program. Really, this can be nothing but a subtle and vicious form of self-will and unbelief.

This is not to imply that God does not sometimes lead us to take positive action, such as writing a letter of inquiry, or letting the right person know that we are interested in a certain type of work. There are normal procedures which are perfectly legitimate for us to follow, unless of course, we are definitely restrained by the Holy Spirit. But anything we do must be open, frank, and aboveboard, rather than underhanded and devious. We don't have to pull wires and play politics and resort to tricks behind the scenes if God is leading us. If the Lord puts in your hand a key to the door, use it. But a key is not a crowbar. If God has given you a key it will fit, and one simple turn will suffice.

Possibly the most important thing to learn in this business of interpreting providence is that when the Lord is leading there will be a steadily unfolding series of circumstantial cues all pointing the same direction. One isolated indication—one open door, no matter how wide—can be misleading. Just as vandals can turn street signs around, so Satan can open a false door at the moment of greatest confusion and weakness. It may look for all the world like the answer to our prayers. It was "the south wind" that "blew softly" that enticed the captain of the ship out of the safe harbor into the driving storm (Acts 27: 7-15). Many a "south wind" has led to shipwreck. A charming person has come into one's life, only later to prove the very emissary of Satan himself. A promising door has swung wide. But if we look carefully we will see that there is something phony about these signposts. They don't jibe with the Map (Scripture) or conscience or with other providential details.

And often we will observe that these false openings will come *just before* the true plan of God is revealed.

A young minister with a wife and three small sons was struggling during the depression to keep food on the table. Knowing also that the district superintendent was about to close his dying church, he was sorely tried. No other church seemed to want him and his little family. At the very height of his perplexity and distress he received a letter from his father-in-law asking him to come home to operate one of his farms. A good house and salary were offered, to say nothing of eggs and milk and all the abundance that the farm offered. And he loved to farm. It looked like the logical way out. Surely God was in this! He was ready to fire back a letter of gleeful acceptance. But he prayed about the matter. That spoiled his delight, for the more he prayed, the worse he felt about it. He couldn't escape the nagging reminder that God had called him to preach. When he wrote to reject the offer, the inward peace told him he had just escaped a trap. Very shortly after that another church called him, leading to many more fruitful years in the full-time ministry.

Counsel. The first sign of headstrong, dangerous fanaticism is unwillingness either to seek counsel from more experienced Christians or to accept it of them. Unfortunately, some get a notion into their heads, take the "bit in their teeth," and dash off on their own way. Perhaps they are seeking to imitate Paul, who "conferred not with flesh and blood" (Gal. 1:16). But this was immediately after the apostle's remarkable conversion and Spirit infilling, and he needed to get alone in the Arabian desert to sort things out. This was not the end of the story, either, for after three years he consulted with Peter and James, the Lord's brother, in Jerusalem (vv. 18-19). Fourteen years later he went again to Jerusalem for the express purpose of communicating with "them which were of reputation, lest by any means I should run, or had run, in vain" (2:2).

A mature Christian, with years of experience in spiritual things, may at times be absolutely sure of his guidance even when it runs contrary to the opinions of his brethren. But young Christians have less reason for this kind of certainty; with them it is more apt to be cockiness. Normally in matters that concern the welfare of the church the Lord leads at both ends of the line. He leads groups, not just individuals. If the Lord is really in our strong impression He will probably give insight to some close friend which will confirm it. If our brethren in whom we have confidence counsel against our proposed action or move, we had better stop and reconsider. It could very well be that we are mistaken.

Reason. Our reasoning faculty is a gift from God and it is our obligation both to cultivate it and use it. At the same time, to rely exclusively on our reason, as if our reason itself were sufficient, is not only pride but folly. Our confidence in our reason exceeds its competence. On the other hand, to feign exclusive guidance of the Holy Spirit by decrying reason is to open the door to fanaticism. For the use of reason is nothing more or less than the practice of the admonition in Eph. 5:15-17: "See then that ye walk circumspectly, not as fools, but as wise, redeeming the time, because the days are evil. Wherefore be ye not unwise, but understanding what the will of the Lord is."

To "walk circumspectly" means to look all around, being alert to all the implications of life. It means to take thoughtfully into consideration all the various factors of every situation insofar as we can perceive them, seeking always the added illumination and perception of the Holy Spirit. It is reason which utilizes the four tests which we have already discussed: Scripture, right, providence, and counsel, and attempts to put them together in a harmonious whole, excluding those ideas and impressions which do not conform to all the tests.

It must be kept in mind also that God's leadings are always intrinsically reasonable, whether the reasonableness is apparent at the moment or not. For example, think again of the preacher who was impressed to stop at the strange house. Even if he had been mistaken, a cautious and courteous approach at a strange house would have resulted in no harm. There was nothing intrinsically unreasonable in the act. But to have felt impressed to stand on his head in the middle of a busy street and yell like the proverbial "Comanche Indian" would have been a doubtful impression indeed. The action would have been intrinsically unreasonable—just as unreasonable as for the mother of six small children to claim that God has told her to leave them and go to Africa as a missionary.

Having insisted on this principle, however, it needs to be reiterated that occasionally guidance comes which seems, at least to some people, to be irrational. E. S. Phillips speaks of this as "unconventional guidance" and suggests as an example Noah building the ark twenty miles from water. But if such guidance is truly of God the rain will come sooner or later. The unfolding of events will vindicate us, rather than expose our folly. It seemed to the mocking neighbors that it was unreasonable for Bud Robinson to profess a call to preach when he couldn't speak without excessive stuttering. But it only *seemed* unreasonable; it was not intrinsically unreasonable. God's seal on his efforts soon proved this fact.

Pitfalls to Be Avoided

Pride. This, of course, is the most deadly peril of all. There are several telltale signs of pride. One is an unwillingness to admit error, and an insistence that God has infallibly guided us in everything we have done. The truth is, the art of successful daily guidance is not learned overnight. It takes years to learn to recognize quickly and accurately the voice of the Holy Spirit in all sorts of strange and confusing situations. In the process of learning there is always a period of what we might call trial and error, involving a certain amount of false moves. The moment we see we are mistaken, we should admit it, and back up and make adjustments if need be. If other people believe we are being misled, we can humbly say that so far as we understand the will of the Lord this is the direction He wants us to go. We can ask an interest in their prayers for further guidance in case we are mistaken. This is a safe attitude to take and the Lord can then more readily reveal by circumstances who is wrong.

Another telltale mark of pride is the supposition that we have a special private "hot line" not available to others. This often gives rise to two further pitfalls:

Domination. When a Christian becomes infatuated with himself and his own private access to special divine guidance, it will be very difficult for him to resist the temptation to use this as a weapon in forcing his will on others. His claim of guidance thus becomes a form of blackmail to compel others to dance to his tune. When he stands up before a group and says, "The Lord told me we should do this," he implies that any disagreement is rebellion against Almighty God. Such a person may be sincere and completely unconscious of his real motivation, but he is seriously misguided. When the Lord is leading, this kind of cracking the whip in the name of the government is not necessary. It has already been pointed out that if the issue involves others, particularly the church, the guidance is not likely to be confined to one person.

Fanaticism. Naturally pride and domination will lead to fanaticism. This consists of irregular conduct or opinions ascribed vociferously to the Holy Spirit but unsubmitted to rational examination and undisciplined by either law or advice. By this stage the infected person is not amenable to appeal or reason. The least criticism of his actions, or the slightest insinuation that he is not acting directly upon orders from above, is branded as an evidence of worldliness and backsliding. He sees himself as the most spiritual person in the involved circle, and the only one whom God can trust with leadership. He rejects quickly any attempt to offer counsel, even from his ecclesiastical superiors, whose duty it is to do so. He acts rashly and precipitately, without due caution and consideration. He is headstrong and stubborn.

It will be surprising if in the development of his fanaticism he does not eventually propose wild notions of doctrine that are insupportable by the Scripture. Sometimes such people are caught in actions or standards of conduct which are immoral, resulting ultimately in the collapse of homes and even the breaking up of churches.

Concluding Rules for Guidance

1. *Don't try to reproduce anyone else's guidance in your life.*

2. *Don't expect everyday occurrences of dramatic guidance,* which you can write about or talk about. Most of our guidance will come in ordinary ways. There will be the gentle pressure of the Holy Spirit upon our spirits and the opening and closing of doors. There will also be the exercise of our judgment after sincere prayer and taking into account the various factors.

3. *Learn experientially the full meaning of Col. 3: 15:* "And let the peace of God rule in your hearts." The word "rule" in this case means arbitrate, which suggests that the peace of God acts as an umpire or arbitrator. Make the decision that is sanctioned by the peace

of God within your heart. Avoid the decisions that do not carry the peace of God with them.

4. *Do not act hastily.* Usually (at least on major matters) the imperious impression that demands immediate action, without time for prayer or thought, is not of God. The Holy Spirit leads gently, patiently, and gives us time to inquire into the true nature and source of the impression. It is Satan who seeks to push Christians into rash action, threatening them that if they do not act right now they will be grieving God and possibly damning some soul.

5. *Do not be too cast down when you have reason to believe that you have missed the Holy Spirit's signal.* If the Holy Spirit has been grieved, He will let you know in a gentle chiding, and you will be grieved too. But He expects you to put the failure "under the Blood," and to learn by the experience so that you may better interpret His voice next time. Then you can go on without needless self-torture and recrimination. It is the devil who cracks the whip, not God. Sometimes one will have an impression to speak to someone about his soul, but will hesitate because the circumstances seem to make the wisdom of a sudden, unconventional approach doubtful. In one's hesitation the opportunity swiftly passes, and is gone. Often Satan then torments the timid and conscientious Christian by unfair accusations. He tries to make him think the failure was caused by a carnal fear of man, a lack of love for souls, or other such serious fault. The truth is that caution in most circumstances is wise. There are, of course, other situations in which the Christian worker must move promptly and decisively. It is expecting too much to suppose that an inexperienced Christian will always be able to know when promptness is wise and when caution is wise. It is in such matters that mistakes will be made, but it is in respect to such mistakes that we may be sure of the

mercy of an understanding Heavenly Father. "Like as a father pitieth his children, so the Lord pitieth them that fear him. For he knoweth our frame; he remembereth that we are dust" (Ps. 103:13-14).

6. *Keep on praying for guidance.* Wait for it to come in all major matters. Cultivate a sensitivity and responsiveness to the pressure of the Spirit even in everyday matters. Above all, be sure to obey when you have that quiet inner conviction that God has spoken.

QUESTIONS FOR DISCUSSION

1. Why is the wholly sanctified believer more apt to experience guidance in his daily life than carnal Christians?

2. Suppose we sincerely believe God is leading us in a certain matter, yet events do not turn out as we expect. Is this an absolute proof that we were mistaken?

3. What if two Christians claim opposite guidance about the same matter? What should be done? Are God's leadings ever diverse with different people about the same thing?

4. What is the difference between "surrendering our preferences" as each new challenge arises and surrendering our *self-willfulness* once for all when we are sanctified?

CHAPTER NINE

The Humanity of the Sanctified

Scriptures for background:

Ps. 103: 1-18; II Cor. 4: 6-18; 12: 7-10; Heb. 13: 3

Having come this far, we should pause and look around. As glorious and satisfying as is the grace of heart holiness, it does not make angels out of us. It does not instantly do everything for us that needs to be done. We are still men, living in physical bodies on a spinning, terrestrial ball called earth. As men we possess the nature of a biological organism, requiring air, water, and food for life, rest for renewal, space for movement. Human nature also includes the God-ordained gifts of reason, self-consciousness, self-direction and freedom of action, sexuality, and such propensities as curiosity and sociality. Sexuality includes the mating, familial, and paternal instincts, plus the distinctive traits of femininity and masculinity. Man is blessed furthermore with vivid imagination, the ability to remember the past and look ahead to the future. He has a capacity for inventiveness and for artistic and mechanical skills. He has a system of values and a sense of beauty and form.

This is man as God created him. In fact Adam was more normally human in all these particulars than we are now. His body was free from disease and his mind unclouded. But sin has blighted the race, so that human nature as we now know it is in poor shape. First it is blighted by an inherited core of sinful selfishness, which we have studied earlier. As we have seen, we may be cleansed from this sinful disposition, so that we can love God with all our being. But human nature has been blighted not only by sin, but by sin's effects. And while the sin may be cleansed, the effects will remain until we receive our glorified bodies in the next life.

What are these effects, or "scars"? One of these is the subjection of our bodies to weariness, pain, disease, and death. Though our bodies are "fearfully and wonderfully made," they are not as highly efficient as we would like or as they were intended to be. Our minds, too, are defective even at the best. In truth, in the words of Paul, "we have this treasure in earthen vessels" (II Cor. 4:7)—and, what is worse, they are badly cracked.

Our feet may be in the path of holiness and service, but they are feet of clay nevertheless. Our minds may think God's thoughts and grasp His truth, but never perfectly. Indeed the measure of accuracy and fullness of understanding we do enjoy is due to the direct aid of the Holy Spirit. Our hearts may burn to speak God's message, but it will come through faltering lips, and often be spoken in words that are limp and weak, maybe even erroneous or unwise. Our hands may be busy about the Master's business, yet fall woefully short in getting the job done.

All of this is true, even with Spirit-filled believers who are living the "life of power." The *treasure* is there. The power is there, constantly available for appropriation—and frequently manifested. But the vessels still are earthen. If we suppose that holiness will be the end of earthiness, we will soon be confused and frustrated. We must learn to distinguish between our earthiness and sin, and then learn to let the indwelling Spirit work through our earthiness—maybe even mend some of the cracks a little. If we do, we will come to see why our very limitations enhance the glory of God: "that the excellency of the power may be of God and not of us."

When we were still in an unsanctified state, it was important that we came to understand our carnality. Now that we have been cleansed, we need to come to an understanding of our *humanity,* particularly in its relation to the sanctified life. (And we must not forget to make plenty of room for the other person's humanity as well as our own.)

The Nuisance of Being Finite

"Remember my bonds," said Paul. He was speaking of his prison chains, but he could have said the same about those limitations inherently his as a man—the kind we all share. We are confined to one spot at a time; we can live only one moment at a time. Time cannot be rerun as a strip of news film. In the exuberance of conversion eager new Christians are apt to forget these bonds and dash off as if they had been given wings. This error is even more likely when believers are exploded into new fervency by the fullness of the Holy Spirit.

Bodies of clay. Undoubtedly it is true that the power of the Spirit quickens the body, often producing a new surge of energy and health, sometimes definite healing. But even a well body has its limits. If in our eagerness to do for God we overspend our physical capital, there is going to be trouble.

One man was thus reckless in his glad, abandoned service as a young, fire-baptized Christian. The hilarity of his spirit smothered any awareness of fatigue. For three years he followed a program of rushing to a service somewhere every night after a hard day of manual labor, then doubling up on Sunday with several services. One Monday morning he tried to bounce out of bed as usual, but couldn't. He found himself trembling and weak. Thereafter he was compelled to limp along in part-time activity, a semi-invalid, and died at an early age of heart exhaustion. It had not occurred to him that holiness had not taken him out of the body, or transformed it from a hunk of clay, easily broken, into its celestial form.

Jesus was seeking to teach this lesson when, after raising the twelve-year-old girl from the dead, He instructed the amazed parents "that something should be given her to eat" (Mark 5:43). That word of common sense brought them back to earth, and helped them to see that, although she was a miracle child, they must not presume on the perpetuation of the miraculous. She had not been made exempt from natural law. If they didn't feed her she would die again, for she was now just as subject to the need of proper food and rest as anyone else.

If holy people forget this, a physical reaction will bring raw nerves and depressed emotions. This is what Satan has been waiting for. Fiendishly he will move in, shooting thick and fast his fiery darts of doubt, temptation, and accusation. Unless a Christian finds out quickly what is happening and why, he will be bewildered, and perhaps be plunged into a period of darkness.

Sometimes the Christian with a chronic ailment not only lives longer, because he learns to live sensibly, but even accomplishes more for God. Simply by being compelled to use wisely every ounce of strength and guard jealously every precious minute, he makes the most of what he has.

Unequal abilities. While some may have to learn the lesson that their bodies are limited, others must discover that their abilities are limited also. They may still be round pegs in square holes in certain church jobs. The Holy Spirit may have put a song in their hearts but has not by virtue of that fact equipped them to sing in the choir. They may now have ten-talent zeal hitched to one-talent gifts. Of course God would far rather have one-talent Christians with ten-talent zeal than to have ten-talent Christians who are smug and lazy. But this is poor consolation to the "eager beaver" who wants to convert the world and then begins cracking his shins and stubbing his toes and banging his head against stone walls. If physical exhaustion tends to depression, *this* induces acute frustration. Some of those stone walls may be *people*—maybe even the organizational restraints of the church. These things that hamper one's free-swinging style like moldy dog-leashes out of Noah's ark can add vexation to frustration. At this point Christians need to have another prayer meeting, and ask God to help them to adjust to reality without losing the fire—and without becoming censorious and sour. Otherwise the problem will become chronic, and we will have one more recruit for the army of "frustrated saints." This army is already too large, and it has yet to win its first battle.

When Holy People Seem Less than Saintly

The Spirit-filled believer loves God with all his heart, soul, mind, and strength and his neighbor as himself. This is the glad inner quality and spontaneous outflow of his life. He has been purged (even in the subconscious) from bitterness, rebelliousness toward God, hatred, envy, covetousness, and worldly-mindedness. He is now conscientious, spiritually-minded, Christ-centered, and is reaching for more and more of God.

But his personality may not yet be a good vehicle of the love within. He may not always seem to convey love. His inner character may be essentially Christlike, but his outward personality may fall short of Christlikeness in some situations. He may have traits which annoy even his best friends, to say nothing of unsaved people who are critical and more readily see the dross than the gold. At times a faulty personality may seriously hinder, in personal relationships, the very thing the holy heart so yearns to accomplish.

Not only so, but sanctified people may be shocked to learn that perfect love does not automatically achieve perfectly smooth and ideal relationships even with other sanctified believers. This discovery sometimes is soul-shaking—almost traumatic. Though the problem of interpersonal relationships in churches, homes, schools, and even on the mission field, is not nearly as severe among the wholly sanctified as among the carnal, it is still there. Unpleasant misunderstandings are still possible. Divine love draws and holds people together, but does not instantly polish the exterior, or avoid the pain of sharp edges and rough surfaces which they may feel in their *very togetherness.*

What are the human factors which make us so different even in holiness that we are sometimes a trial and enigma to each other? What is this residue of faults in our personalities which misrepresents Jesus and therefore still needs to be removed—or at least disciplined?

Masculinity and femininity. When we were children we sang, "What are little girls made of?" and the answer invariably was, "Sugar and spice and all things nice." When the same question was asked about boys, the answer was not nearly so flattering. Actually the difference is not that bad. There is really no advantage either way. The advantage lies in the fact that there *are* real differences. Woman could hardly meet man's need as a helpmeet if she were just like him. It is fortunate that woman is intuitive, perceptive, finely tuned to human suffering, and has great capacity for detail. But above all lie the traits of courage and endurance. Her tear ducts are her safety valve for both joy and sorrow. She feeds on affection, security, stability, and tenderness, but gives all this in return with double measure.

The masculine nature is geared to achievement and conquest, and desperately needs the support of an understanding wife. The man's shortcoming is that he does not always know how to give this understanding in return. Cut on coarser, more rugged lines, he sees the big issues, and is sometimes heedless of the little things that mean so much to a woman. Because of these differences (and many more) a husband and wife, even though sanctified, may be a puzzle to each other at times. In fact—we may as well admit it—they may even be a trial to each other. This is particularly true in the early years, when they both make many blunders, and sometimes wound unintentionally through nothing in the world but lack of understanding. The humility, adaptability, sincerity, and teachableness so necessary to keep sanctified are also the essentials for overcoming the problems inherent in masculine-feminine differences.

Temperament and temper. One's temperament is his natural pattern of action and reaction. By nature one may tend to be quick while another may be slow. One is emotionally excitable; one is sluggish. We feel like dowsing the one with a bucket of water and building a fire under the other. When a racehorse disposition is teamed up with a workhorse either in marriage, on the church board, or wherever, the harness will be put to a severe strain. The one will be popping with ideas, will want to dash into new schemes right now, and will have little patience for dolts and laggards. The other will be methodical, cautious, and analytical. They need each other, but they will experience times when it is hard for them to believe it.

Psychologists talk about extroverts, introverts, and ambiverts. Extroverts are those who express themselves with a minimum of inhibitions. They are sociable, communicative, warm. The introverts live within themselves, are thoughtful, sensitive, shy. Sometimes these two groups are further subdivided into the choleric, sanguine, melancholic, and phlegmatic temperaments. The first is volatile; the second is cheerful and optimistic; the third is pessimistic; the fourth is unemotional. These adjectives, of course, so completely oversimplify the picture that they might better be omitted. But the types are all around us, nevertheless, and generally on every church board. Basic temperament will tend to mold the way the respective board members look at the same problem even when all are equally spiritual. The sanguine will rush into a building program too soon; the choleric (in spite of grace) may show signs of impatience and excitability; the melancholic will magnify all the difficulties; the phlegmatic will never get "worked up" but may have the best judgment in the end. Incidentally, it is the pastor who will get the ulcers.

Excitability, of itself, is not necessarily carnal temper. When debating an issue rather warmly a phlegmatic missionary said to another, "Control your temper!" Whereupon the other retorted, "I control more temper in a day than you do in a year." It is ugly, selfish, petty, and uncontrollable "temper" that is purged when the temper itself (properly defined) is sanctified wholly. But even when sanctified, there will not always be perfect emotional poise. Only Jesus had that. Spontaneous reactions may be rooted both in love and in temperament; therefore may be pure while at the same time hasty and unwise. Sometimes they will require apology.

Fortunately most of us are ambiverts; that is, we have the traits of both extroverts and introverts in reasonable balance. Not only so, but extreme imbalance in either direction can be modified by grace and discipline. The hasty person can learn to think before he speaks and look before he leaps. And certainly no mature person would permit himself to be "temperamental." That is the mark of a selfish and spoiled person. But in spite of grace, discipline, and maturity, the basic characteristics of natural temperament will always cling to us, as the framework of our style of personality.

Emotional immaturity. A sanctified Christian may have signs in his personality of emotional immaturity. This weakness does not consist necessarily in a tendency to show or express emotion. At times, it is true, the ability to hide emotion can be a mark of adulthood, if the situation demands that true feelings be hid. A wedding is not exactly the time for the mother of the bride to collapse in uncontrolled weeping, for instance. But in most situations, normal emotion should be expressed, while not hysterically, yet frankly and unashamedly.

But the real mark of immaturity is the tendency to extremes of emotion not justified by the occasions which prompt them. Examples would be an excessive gaiety or an excessive grief over mere trifles. We expect a child to weep over a lost teddy bear because he is a child. But when the child becomes a man or a woman we expect a more grown-up, sensible sense of values. Tears must not be permitted to be as copious over broken dishes as over broken lives. Getting one's hair exactly right is not as important as getting to church on time. Having the latest gadget, or the best sports equipment, is not as important as paying our bills and having a savings account. An expensive, purse-flattening hunting trip that we rationalize as being "needed" is not as important as financial solvency and vocational reliability. The "crime" of forgetting a wedding anniversary ought not to plunge a young wife into inconsolable grief. It is not as if her husband had been unfaithful to her. Mature people are known as such by their ability to sort the important from the trivial, and to react emotionally as each experience deserves. This maturity is also an ability to keep even justifiable emotion from so unhinging us that we are unable to fill our role as responsible adults.

Entire sanctification imparts a big shove toward maturity, but only toward it. Holiness, we must remind ourselves again, does not put old heads on young shoulders. Intelligence plays a part here and maturation plays its part also. It is life itself, however, which contributes the lion's share. Meanwhile let us be patient with people who profess to be sanctified, yet at times seem to see things through childish eyes.

Cultural variations. Some, because of educational and social advantages, are refined and possess cultivated taste in clothes, music, art, and literature. Others, even when Spirit-filled, may be handicapped by many crudities and a certain amount of unconscious coarseness. If holy within, they will have the hearts of true gentlemen or ladies, but they may not have been taught the manners. They may therefore possess a certain boisterousness, and unintentional rudeness or awkwardness in delicate social situations. This may reflect on one's background, but not necessarily on one's state of grace. Yet these faults can be annoying, even repelling. It is hard to understand how a wealth of religion can at times be combined with such poverty of social sense and tact.

Holy people may fail to understand each other (and therefore to appreciate each other) on the aesthetic level also. For example, the gospel songs which will bring blessing in one part of the country may be a trial in another. When a certain congregation blessed the Lord by a time of bright chorus singing, the evangelist stood and said dourly: "You need never expect revival as long as you indulge in those frivolous ditties." But it is doubtful whether he really had the mind of the Spirit. He was just reflecting his own cultural prejudices. Fortunately the Holy Spirit is able to adapt himself to various cultures better than some of us are.

The potential misunderstanding can be even more serious when the cultural differences are not only provincial but racial and national. Paul Orjala reports that it is hard for the Haitians, who live in a "face-to-face" culture, to understand an American's desire for privacy, or his concern to protect his possessions. To them, this seems like selfishness and appears irreconcilable with holiness. It is in such ways, multiplied manyfold from race to race and country to country, that misunderstandings can so easily arise. These can threaten the perfection which should mark the fellowship of holy people.

Infirmities. When Jesus rebuked Peter, James, and John for sleeping while He prayed, He added a word of sympathetic understanding: "The spirit indeed is willing, but the flesh is weak." In this case Jesus was referring to their infirmity. The term embraces all those weaknesses of the body and of the mind which are the scars of sin, but which are not in themselves sin. To be overpowered by sleep when excessively weary is not sin; but it can be very embarrassing when one is trying to stay awake during a night of prayer. It can be downright disastrous when driving. The spirit fights to stay awake and the body fights to sleep. This may be just plain nature, not even an infirmity. But when middle-aged people go through an abnormal period when it is almost impossible to stay awake in a Sunday morning service, they have an infirmity on their hands.

Paul dubs his "thorn in the flesh" an infirmity (II Cor. 12:7-10). There is some evidence that this thorn could have been weak eyes, or possibly a tendency to stutter. But whatever it was, it made Paul one with all the saints who have served God in spite of physical and mental handicaps.

What is important for us to see right now is that infirmities adversely affect the personality, and sometimes are the cause and explanation of annoying faults which don't quite "stack up" with our ideal of Christian perfection. Some apparent "symptoms" of carnality may in certain persons have their roots, not in a sinful condition, but in an infirm condition. Poor hearing may cause elderly people to be a bit supersensitive and imaginative. Hardening of the arteries, high blood pressure, and such ailments of the aging, may cause personality deterioration. Raw, taut nerves, due to strain and overwork, may make a person jumpy, even edgy and irritable in extreme situations.

All of us have too many *mental* infirmities for our comfort—poor judgment, poor memory, sluggish comprehension. Take the memory, for instance. Important details of a conversation or an event become hazy. This, coupled with the fact that we are not trained observers in the first place, may result in gross inaccuracy in reporting the past. Two equally sanctified people may disagree radically in describing the same event or recalling the same conversation. Neither one could be accused of lying. It is just that mental infirmity has distorted the picture.

In all these ways (and many more) sanctified people, in their spiritual immaturity, may have minor trouble in getting along with each other. Unsympathetic outsiders may find cause for criticism in such behavior. Man looks on the outward appearance, but fortunately God looks on the heart.

What can be done about this?

Improving the Personality

During the past twenty years the market has been flooded with books on positive thinking, influencing people and making friends, et cetera, ad infinitum. Hundreds of courses have been offered on becoming a more dynamic and successful person. Much can be learned from these media of instruction. But the appeal, too often, is to purely selfish considerations. A bright, personable young man disembarked from a ship in Kobe, Japan, in order to spend three months wandering about Japan on his own. When asked what his purpose was he replied, "Oh, I guess just to make myself a more interesting person." But this motivation is not good enough for the Christian. His constant desire is (1) to be a *better* person, and (2) to be a more *useful* person; and both for Jesus' sake, not just for his own. In becoming more useful it may become necessary for some of us to become more interesting, but this can never be our real goal.

What we are now talking about is the elimination of those faults which hinder our witness as Christians, especially Christians who profess to have experienced Pentecost. We desire not only to be entirely sanctified in the sense of being entirely the Lord's and entirely free from the double-mindedness of the carnal state, but progressively sanctified in the sense of an enlarged and more accurate Christlikeness in personality and understanding. The image of Jesus which we present to those about us must be more faithful in details. In short, we want to get rid not only of every "spot" of sin but our human "wrinkles" as well (Eph. 5:27, NASB). We need a lot of "pressing and ironing" as well as cleansing. But just as a wrinkle is not a dirt spot, so these faults which need to be ironed out in our personalities are not sins.

Of course the chief Agent in this process is the Holy Spirit. He takes the raw material of life—its shocks and blows and sorrows plus unpleasant people—and transforms it into life's emery wheel. When a certain Christian of much experience gave a shrewd answer to a man in a conversation about religion, he said, "You are a smooth article, aren't you!" To which she replied, "Why shouldn't I be?—the Lord's been sandpapering me for thirty years."

Let us not pray for more patience unless we really mean it. The Lord can't give us a neatly wrapped box of patience as a Christmas gift. Patience can exist only when there is something to be patient about. You don't exhort a child to be "patient" when he is happily opening his birthday presents; you rather exhort him to be patient when he wants to open them beforehand. If God humored us as some parents indulge their children, the acquirement of patience would be impossible, as there would be nothing to call for its exercise. And how dwarfed and undeveloped we would be if the people around us were all perfect! But we can console ourselves in knowing that, while they are being used by the Spirit to sandpaper us, we are providing excellent sandpaper for them!

How does the Spirit thus work?

1. *By deepening our love for Jesus and our passion to be like Him.* His success here, of course, depends on the depth and virility of our devotional life.

2. *By helping us to come to terms with our limitations.* Some people make themselves and others unhappy because they are forever restless for jobs that are just a little beyond them. Naturally we grow and develop so that a job which is beyond us today may not be beyond us ten years from now. But some of us never will be qualified for some of the things we would like to do. We may never sing like A, or preach like B, or teach like C, or win souls like D, or minister like E, or sparkle in conversation like F, or think profoundly like G, or make a big first impression like H—but let's stop enumerating right now. To want to do something as well as somebody else can be both stimulating and dangerous. It is stimulating if it inspires us to pay the price for improvement, but it is dangerous if it leads to envy and excessive self-depreciation. We need to put on the altar the great gulf that is fixed between our talents and another's, and never permit ourselves to look across that gulf with envious eyes. Admiration is all right, but not envy.

The art of accepting oneself is one of the fine arts of life. Let us not backslide by hiding our talent in the ground. Let us rather determine to be the cheeriest, most contented, reliable, and productive one-talent Christians of which we are capable.

Not only limited abilities, but limited health, limited finances, and limited opportunities may circumscribe us. But these need not sour us nor defeat us. "Little is much when God is in it."

3. *By helping us to capitalize on our infirmities.* The neurotic or hypochondriac exploits his infirmities to the indulgence of his own selfishness. But the Christian must resolutely seek special resources of divine grace. When the Lord assured Paul that His "strength is made perfect in weakness," this devoted apostle exclaimed: "Most gladly therefore will I rather glory in my infirmities, that the power of Christ may rest upon me" (II Cor. 12:9).

But before this he prayed for deliverance from the thorn. This is also legitimate. Passive, stoical, do-nothing indifference is no proof of superior piety. It is our duty to change what we can. If we have infirmities which we suspect are the cause of a personality defect, or which in any way hinder the work of God and limit our usefulness, it is our duty to at least pray about them. If medical or professional means are available for their correction, such should be used. If training and effort can improve our judgment or memory, or remove an annoying mannerism, we should resolutely engage the remedy.

But if every effort fails, and after persistent prayer God says no, then let us offer these very infirmities to God. He can make us a blessing in spite of them, in some cases even turn them into assets. Uncle Bud Robinson's inability to pronounce his *s*'s was an infirmity, but what an endearing one it became—a sort of hallmark! God did not heal Annie Johnson Flint, but enabled her, through grace, lying helpless on her back, pushing a pencil against a board above her face, to write beautiful and inspiring poems. They probably never would have been written had the religion of "health, wealth, and prosperity" been true and she had been made a well woman. Among her most-loved poems is this one:

> *God hath not promised skies always blue,*
> *Flower-strewn pathways all our lives through;*
> *God hath not promised sun without rain,*
> *Joy without sorrow, peace without pain.*
>
> *But God hath promised strength for the day,*
> *Rest for the labor, light for the way,*
> *Grace for the trials, help from above,*
> *Unfailing sympathy, undying love.*

4. *By imparting to us understanding* (Eph. 1:18; II Tim. 2:7). It is always wise to pray: "Lord, make me an understanding person." More than half the battle in interpersonal relationships is won when we understand one another. This is true with husbands and wives, missionaries and preachers, pastors and parishioners, employers and employees. Communication is the key.

Some of this understanding may be acquired only by frank, face-to-face talking. Then talk! Don't talk behind a person's back, then tell him to his face that nothing is wrong. Don't let silence drive wedges of ever deepening misunderstanding and suspicion between you and others.

Some of this understanding can be gleaned from study—the Bible, psychology, reliable books. In the process you will be supplying your "virtue" (zeal) with "knowledge" (II Pet. 1:5), and thus:

a. *You will come gradually to understand the difference between carnality and humanity.* In Chapter Two we talked about the "believer's failure," and in that discussion we meant *sin*. We described his failure to experience that love for God and man which is the

New Testament standard. This failure is rooted in the carnal mind, and is a failure which may be eliminated in the grace of heart holiness. Now we seem to be talking about failure again; only this time we are calling it infirmity, or humanity. It does seem confusing, admittedly, especially when some of the personality faults may seem so similar to those which are seen in unsanctified Christians.

But the Spirit will help us to see that in God's sight —who alone knows the heart perfectly—there is a vast difference qualitatively between, say, a mother's anxiety for the spiritual welfare of her children and the anxiety over the superior popularity of a rival; or between overwork in unwise zeal for the Lord and overwork striving for material possessions; or between the stubbornness of a surrendered will and the stubbornness of an unsurrendered will. The fact that one may be mistaken, and unable at the moment to distinguish between God-given, Bible-based convictions and man-made, hand-me-down notions, does not discount the purity of one's heart. And so the examples could be multiplied.

b. The Spirit will help you to understand yourself. This will save you from confusion and discouragement, or worse yet, from throwing away your confidence, when your reactions do not measure up to your ideals. Is everything still "on the altar"? Do you love God with all your heart? Your neighbor? Is there no ill will, envy, unforgiving spirit, malice, deceit, bitterness, rebelliousness, unbelief, worldly-mindedness, or covetousness? These are the telltale shoots of sin. If the Lord shows you no such positive evidences of a sinful condition, then hold steady in both faith and profession, in spite of wobbly feelings and edginess. But at the same time let the Spirit show you what He is at the moment trying to teach you. Then you may need to make adjustments in your living habits to recapture the poise and joys of a trustful, relaxed pace. And you may have to make adjustments with *people* whom you may have unintentionally hurt. But make the adjustments—then go on!

c. *You will gain understanding of the personality needs of others.* Don't scorn people who seem to want more than their share of attention. Maybe they need it. Some people are emotionally starved, others emotionally exhausted. Some are groping to find themselves. They need praise, recognition, and reassurance from us during these difficult times of uncertainty and anxiety. Such needs are especially acute during adolescence, young adulthood, and old age.

d. *The Holy Spirit will keep adjusting the focus of your outlook on life by reminding you repeatedly concerning what is truly important.* A young Chinese friend lives by the slogan: "It doesn't matter." In childhood she was at times hungry, alone, and in danger. Now, against that background, it is easy to keep petty details in healthy perspective! It doesn't really matter if you win the game or not—if you get your name in the church bulletin—if someone else is thanked publicly for work you did—if your motion doesn't carry in the board meeting—if you miss this bus—if that other driver gets ahead of you—if the merchandise you ordered is not delivered on schedule—if you don't get your way in that family discussion. Nothing really matters but God and love and holiness and heaven—and helping others get there. This kind of perspective is absolutely essential if we are to maintain good-humored poise in the rough-and-tumble of everyday life.

What many people do not realize is that after sanctification we are still ourselves, and therefore, as free persons, making fresh decisions every day. Dozens of little nagging events can occur in the course of a week, in the home, at the factory or office or school, or even in the church, which could disturb us dangerously if we would let them. Each one requires us to *decide* whether our attitude will be right or wrong. Satan is constantly seeking to inject the virus of indignation for personal injustices, then cultivate an infection of self-pity and of brooding. To change the figure: when first stung by the nettles of life, the Spirit-filled person can easily handle the crisis. But if he accepts Satan's magnifying glass and focuses on the sore point too long, he will have a severe burn to cope with. This is one of the ways sanctified people become unsanctified. We must learn to commit some things to the Lord, quickly.

Summary

Let us summarize the way the Holy Spirit works in our lives:

1. He instantaneously *cleanses* our carnality, and eliminates from our personality its ugly manifestations.

2. He gradually *corrects* our faults and complexes which are not sinful, but which rise out of our temperament, childhood experiences, infirmities, and human limitations.

3. He *helps* our infirmities at times by healing, at other times by daily assistance, as, for instance, in prayer (Rom. 8:26).

4. He *disciplines* and directs our basic humanity, with its propensities, drives, needs, and appetites.

In Chapter Four we saw that God's method of dealing with indwelling sin was eradication, not suppression or counteraction. Now we see wherein these rejected terms are admissible. Our sin is eradicated, our infirmity is counteracted, our humanity is disciplined and directed, and our bodies may at times have to be just plain *suppressed.* (Remember how Paul put it—I Cor. 9:27?)

But this is a suppression which in the end preserves expression. Unlawful expression leads to a loss of life's powers. But Spirit-prompted suppression expands the powers. The right kind of suppression (or vigorous restraint and control of the natural man) will result, not in impoverishment, but in the healthy fulfillment of the total person. This is the aim and inevitable reward of *life in the Spirit.*

QUESTIONS FOR DISCUSSION

1. Can growth in divine love be cultivated directly or will such growth be the indirect result of cultivating our devotional life?

2. Is the grace of perfect love ever inadequate to keep "incompatible" people together in families and churches?

3. Would you say that a *growing sensitivity* both to the leadings of the Spirit and to the needs of others is one of the surest evidences of heart holiness? What if the years reveal no such growing sensitivity?

4. In what ways has the usefulness of sanctified people been unnecessarily limited by "zeal without knowledge"? Is there danger that in the process of acquiring knowledge we lose our zeal, and become overly cautious and conservative? How can we avoid this?

5. In seeking to improve our personalities do we need at the same time to be constantly guarding the purity of our motives and objectives? Or will this automatically take care of itself?

CHAPTER TEN

The Ethics of Holiness
—Biblical Principles

Scriptures for background:
Psalms 15; Matthew 5:1-16; Romans 12:9-21; 13:1-10

It has already been emphasized that God charges with sin only when He sees wrongness in the heart—in attitudes or intentions. Heart purity is, to use a phrase of the theologian Soren Kierkegaard, "to will one thing." But there is a peril is assuming that, because good intentions are of first importance, the success or failure of our good intentions in actually achieving right conduct is of no consequence. When we find ourselves saying, "I meant well," and let it go at that, with an air that says everybody should accept my good intentions and ignore my wrong actions, we know that we have fallen into this error. To the person who has been hurt by my "well-intended" actions this easy brush-off may seem like a rather shabby evasion of my responsibility. We need to see that such "good intentions" are not as good as they pose. Actually they are seriously defective if they are not aimed in all seriousness at being so thoroughly *right* that both the welfare of people and the honor of God are secured. The possessor of such intentions will therefore be neither careless nor flippant. The chief concern will be that all the details of living will conform to the ethical standards of the Bible.

THE RELATION OF HOLINESS TO ETHICS

Some built-in advantages. We have a right to expect that holy people are consciously, deliberately, and consistently practicing the highest standard of ethics they know. They may be mistaken about the wrongness or rightness of this or that, but they are not aware of the mistake. Things they know to be wrong, they avoid. Things which they believe are right, they practice. Careless, slipshod ethics, combined with a defiance of church rules and accepted standards, simply do not tally with the profession of the grace of entire sanctification. What is more, to persist in unethical practices, whether in business, home, church, or society, proves that the profession is phony. Every truly sanctified man has not only an inbuilt, spontaneous desire to live right and set a good example, but a solid determination to do so.

Furthermore we have a right to expect that a holy person will be anxious to improve in the practical details of Christian living. A genuine experience of holiness will give a teachable spirit. The "wisdom that is from above," James says, is not only pure, but "easy to be intreated" (Jas. 3:17). If you say to any sanctified man: "Brother, this which you are doing is a stumbling block, and is not consistent with Bible standards," he will instantly be concerned. He does not want his life to be a hindrance to anyone. He will not persistently ignore the advice unless he becomes convinced on the basis of the Scriptures that you are mistaken. This attitude is indispensable to an experience of heart holiness. Holiness and lowliness are twins, it has been said, but holiness and arrogance are not.

A sanctified man is conscientious. If not, he is a fake. He is conscientious about his work, his word, his obligations, his family duties. He is conscientious as a Christian steward, as a citizen, as a debtor, as a tax payer, as a car driver, as an employer, or as an employee. The man who professes holiness but has no conscience about observing the law of the land, or being meticulously careful in his tax returns, or in his conduct with the opposite sex, or in maintaining his church vows, is simply self-deceived. His brand of "holiness" is not the kind that will stand Bible inspection.

The limitations. On the basis of these rather severe statements one might suppose therefore that all sanctified people are faultless in their ethics. This would be what logicians call a *non sequitor*—"it does not follow." What is declared, dogmatically and unequivocally, is that sanctified people want to be above reproach in their daily lives, and are striving to that end. It does not follow that their insight always matches their intention. On the whole, holiness people live more consistently exemplary lives than non-holiness people (and this the world has a perfect right to expect). The reason is simply that their heart experience imparts a sharper sensitivity to sin and a more penetrating perception of ethical issues. But even so, in the beginning days this will not be perfect. They may for a while have ethical "blind spots." One's sense of right and wrong may still need straightening out at some points even after one is born again and filled with the Spirit. Entire sanctification does not instantly and automatically educate the conscience.

The Salvation Army folk love to tell of a certain London plumber who was converted under the preaching of Evangeline Booth. After a week he came to her saying, "Ma'am, you don't know what it means to me to be saved. I don't know how to thank you for bringing me to me senses. I wish I had a lot of money to give you." Then with the same simple eagerness he said, "I'll tell you what I can do: I can fix your gas meter so it won't register." We smile at that, for none of us are so naive as to miss what seems to us to be a rather obvious unethical idea. But it was not so to him—yet.

The clear-cut lines of proper conduct (which are observed by all decent, law-abiding citizens) we see clearly enough. It is the fine lines and the light shadings that sometimes confuse us. We easily read the big print in our ethical contract but sometimes need spectacles to see the fine print. In this world of taxes, corporations, dividends, overtime, fringe benefits, coffee breaks, insurance laws, easy divorce, traffic laws, time payments, lawsuits, business protocol, et cetera, life can become very complicated indeed. In the confused array ethical ambiguities can arise which would puzzle a Solomon. Is "fudging" on the coffee break basically any different from fixing a gas meter so it won't register? Or is a practice justified simply because "everybody else in the office does it"?

The possibility of fuzziness in ethical perception is augmented by the breakdown in moral standards in society at large. Many people have a very warped sense of "honor." The proverbial "honor among thieves" is matched by the confused adults who would rather steal and rob than to "disgrace" themselves by accepting menial jobs. Where honor has been sharply defined, as at the United States Air Force Academy ("I will not lie, cheat, or steal, or tolerate anyone who does"), the standard has met with a shockingly widespread protest. Even more revealing of our muddled thinking than the cheating of the cadets (discovered in early 1965) was the reaction of the parents in defending, not the Academy, but the cheaters.

Our concern right now is that this prevailing tendency to blur the lines between right and wrong can creep into the thinking of good people. It finds its way into holiness colleges and churches. For many people there is still a need for guidance in sound Christian ethics and for vigorous Bible study in this area.

When Black Seems White

When we are in a complicated life-situation we discover that ethical problems and strong temptations have one thing in common: their peril is in their deceptiveness. If we can see the thing as it really is, we will (if our hearts are right) do the right. But Satan is a master in playing on our emotions and confusing the issues so that we see a distorted picture. He can make the lesser appear the greater, and the greater seem the lesser. He can make compromise seem like innocent expediency. He will annoy us with trifles in order to divert our attention from important issues. He knows that a fact out of perspective is equivalent to a falsehood, so he works on our perspective. In all these ways he seeks to make right appear wrong and wrong seem right.

The problem is complicated by the fact that our humanity sometimes comes to the devil's aid. It is hard to think clearly when we are emotionally involved. Natural affections can fog one's vision. Parents, for example, can easily see the wrongness in the conduct of other youth but are often blind to the wrongness of identical conduct in their own. Or our financial interests may prompt actions or attitudes which seem justified in the highly electric tension of the moment, but which later we perceive to be less than ethical. Were we completely honest in that car deal, or in the selling of the house, or trading the old washer for a new one, or giving our medical history when applying for insurance? In all these matters, are we Christians first and traders and property owners second? Or is the reverse true?

Not that we intend any wrongdoing. But under emotional pressure some things seem like "just good sense" which may, when seen in a better light, be discovered to be better "sense" than religion.

How can we always be sure of perceiving what is right? There is only one way. We must stand every ethical situation up against the plumb line of God's Word. This requires two things: First we must know God's Word. Secondly, we must follow God's Word, rather than our own judgment or anyone else's. Our judgment may be warped, but God's Word is forever the same. When God says a thing is wrong we must believe that it is wrong, without stopping to question. It makes no difference whether every voice in the world, including the voice of our own reason and all five senses, contradicts God.

If Eve had observed this simple rule, the Fall would not have occurred. Astounding thought! When Satan, through the serpent, succeeded in calling into question God's word, he was assured of the outcome. Satan's master strategy was in suggesting that God's word was not to be taken literally. God didn't really mean *that*—so let's take a look and see what modifications we can make and still be religious. Having already sinned in her heart by accepting the doubt, the next step for Eve was to study the tree for herself, to see if what the devil said was true. In this act she was abandoning the simple word of God as her rule of action and substituting her own senses and her own judgment. This is always the process in a "fall." Man falls when he ceases to say, "This is what God says," and begins to say, "This is the way it looks to me."

In the stress of a crucial moment, our own judgment, pushed and tugged at by the crosscurrents of our emotions, desires, and senses, plus the opinions of others, is incompetent as a sure judge of right and wrong. We must know the Word of God, and fall back upon it, as

Jesus did in the wilderness. God has commanded some things, and forbidden others. Then let those things be forever settled. The Christian who would be safe must say, "If God in His Word pronounces this wrong, then it is wrong for me, whether I am able to see anything wrong in it or not." Therefore let the commandment to honor our parents settle for us the problem of what to do with the old folks. Let the sixth commandment, illuminated by the Sermon on the Mount and the First Epistle of John, keep us reminded that hatred, ill will, and an unforgiving spirit are forever wrong. So also are all practices destructive of life and limb or health. If we resolutely go right down the line, many patches of cloudiness in our thinking will disappear. We can at least trace out the clear, bold lines drawn in the Word of God. About these there can be no excuse. Fidelity to one's mate is demanded from Genesis to Revelation. A tolerated polygamy in Old Testament times is forced to yield before the unmistakable teaching of Christ and the apostles that monogamy is the norm of nature. This was the original intention of God and it is the Christian standard. Impurity in any form is irreconcilable with Christian discipleship, as are also revelling, drunkenness, quarreling, reviling, lying, stealing, and any of the practices which Paul included in his two ultimatums in I Cor. 6:8-10 and Gal. 5:21. They who do such things, the apostle warned, shall not "inherit the kingdom of God."

Letting Love Draw the Lines

But the Christian needs to know not only the clear, bold lines which govern the grosser forms of evil, but the scriptural principles which will guide him in the delicate situations wherein the right is obscured. Sometimes the arguments on both sides seem to be balanced. "On the one hand . . . but on the other hand"—our very conscientiousness will lead us into this trap. We can get out by remembering that there is a new ingredient in

New Testament ethics called "the second mile." When the law itself is ambiguous we can let love take over. Love will clarify much murkiness that law leaves untouched. After all, love, and love alone, is the dynamic of Christian ethics. It is both the motivating drive and the arbiter. The judgment still may make a mistake, but judgment steered by law plus love is far more apt to strike it right than judgment ruled by law alone. For love in its very essence is seeking the highest welfare of the other person. This is what it means to love our neighbor as ourselves. It is this or nothing. Therefore love is willing to settle some issues in the other fellow's favor even when justice might not demand it, and go the second mile even when law might not require it. This is why the Christian motivated by perfect love will think not only of the Ten Commandments but certain other scriptures, and take them very seriously. Let us survey quickly a few of these passages, without too much attempt at classification.

1. Matt. 7:12: *Whatsoever ye would that men should do to you, do ye even so to them.* This we know as the golden rule. It insists on the principle of *fairness.* In many respects this is the acid test of Christian ethics, and this idea of fairness is implicit in most of the other verses which we will examine. Let us therefore take a second look here.

One value in well-organized and disciplined sports is the sense of fair play imbibed by the participants—at least to the extent that even a "Little Leaguer" is quick to see when the *other* fellow is unfair! But in sports, love is not the dynamic in the achievement of fairness, hence rules and officials must be resorted to. But the sole aim of rules is fairness. That which makes a "foul" *foul* is its intrinsic unfairness to one's opponent. The golden rule helps us distinguish between fairness and unfairness by suggesting that we ask a simple question: How would I like to be treated in this situation? If I have, on an impulse, made a thoughtless, indiscreet remark which could get me into trouble if repeated, would I want my friend to quote me? Then neither should I tell that "juicy morsel" which might embarrass him. Do I desire men to be truthful with me? To keep their word? To be fair with me? Do I desire my wife (or husband) to be loyal to me? Do I want others to be patient with me, to forgive me when I ask, and overlook my many shortcomings even when I don't ask? Do I desire men to be generous in their estimate of my motives, and give me the benefit of the doubt? Then all of this I should do to others.

There is a surprise element in the golden rule, however. When I ask myself how I would *like* to be treated in a certain situation I am assuming that I have a right to be treated in the way I would like. Suppose I *deliberately* run a red light. I might "like" for the officer to be lenient, but in my heart I will despise both him and myself if I succeed in talking him into treating me as I might like. When Jesus gave us the rule, therefore, He did not intend to authorize unlimited leniency on all sides. In applying the golden rule we need to assume a few extra words: "Whatsoever therefore ye would that men should do to you, in the light of all the circumstances, the preservation of right and the public welfare, do ye even so to them." When I think like this I know that I want a lot of mercy, but not totally at the expense of justice, for this wouldn't even be in my own best interests in the long run. If I am honest in this kind of thinking I won't have too much trouble in deciding on what is fair for the other man. There will be justice softened by mercy, but never mere license or unbridled leniency.

2. Rom. 13:10a: *Love worketh no ill to his neighbour.* The Ten Commandments forbid certain actions because those actions are not only unfair but injurious. They hurt others. In some way they deprive their vic-

tims of some God-given right. They are actions which meanly obstruct someone in his pursuit of life, liberty, and happiness. Love is the master key that fits all such laws, simply because love will not knowingly harm its object in any way. "Therefore love is the fulfillment of the law." On the surface this verse may seem like a faulty statement of the case, for it seems to be satisfied with a mere negative harmlessness. On this basis many people would roundly declare their virtue, for are they not forever professing that they "never hurt anybody"? But their concept of "hurting" is too narrow. The world is full of "harmless" neighbors who do not know that failing to do good may be the most devastating form of "working ill." Many parents have worked irremediable ill to their children by neglecting their souls. They supposed they were exhausting their duty by feeding, clothing, and educating them. Many church members have worked ill by their silence in times of moral crisis. Many others have sinned eternally against their neighbors by saying not one word to them about the Saviour. No, true love is never content simply with negative harmlessness. It avoids working ill by doing well: by seeking to be helpful in time of need and, above all, to be redemptive.

3. Rom. 12:17b: *Provide things honest in the sight of all men.* The Greek word which is here translated "honest" means much more than bare legality. It goes beyond the kind of honesty that merely gives full measure of goods and pays the bill to the penny. The word means *honorable*. The world may see a Christian as perfectly honest, but nevertheless mean and miserly. His business deals may be legal, yet still more like those of Shylock than of Christ. Our standard, therefore, is not merely legality, but magnanimity. It goes beyond the letter of the law, overflows with warmth and generosity, and yields the advantage cheerfully rather than grasping it grimly.

4. I Cor. 10:31: *Whether therefore ye eat, or drink, or whatsoever ye do, do all to the glory of God.* Most of us do not take this passage seriously enough. It is actually the foundation of all else. The Christian is to be honorable in the sight of men, not that honor shall accrue to him, but to his Lord. For the "glory" of God (in this case) is the honor of God. What do our eating and drinking habits have to do with the honor of God? How can what we eat either diminish or augment in the least the mighty name of God? It cannot among angels, but it can among men, and it is magnifying God's honor among men that is to be our aim. Wrong living dishonors God and brings shame and reproach on His name before His enemies. When Paul chided the Jews, "For the name of God is blasphemed among the Gentiles through you" (Rom. 2:24), he meant that their inconsistent conduct turned their noble and divinely given religion into a laughingstock. Christians may also become guilty of bringing dishonor upon the name of God.

In seeking God's honor among men, everything has a bearing. Nothing is unimportant, not even our eating. If our personal habits cheapen us as Christians, or cause others to stumble, or in any way make Jesus Christ and His holy way repugnant and unattractive, then those habits are not for the glory of God. No matter how trifling therefore a practice seems to be, it ceases to be trifling the moment it is seen to be related to God's glory. It becomes then gravely important, with an importance reflected from the majestic name which it either enhances or tarnishes.

Recently a pastor confessed a humiliating experience which became a milestone in his spiritual life. When he learned that a member of his church was using tobacco he went to him and kindly sought to instruct him. He was thoroughly squelched by the man's retort: "Pastor, I suppose you are right. But I will listen more willingly when you set a better example. Time and again I have watched you at a potluck dinner heap your plate high, then go back and heap it again, eating far more than is good for you. Is not that abusing the body too?" The pastor went home to pray, and set the house of his own personal habits in order. The result was better health, a trimmer figure, a more disciplined character, and far greater moral authority as a spiritual leader. Then he went back to his tobacco-using member, this time with success.[1]

5. I Cor. 6:20: . . . *glorify God therefore in your body*. Not only is the glory of God to be our aim in whatever we do, but our bodies are to be the means by which this aim is to be achieved. Therefore the body is sacred. But its sacredness is double: not only can it be used to serve the Lord, but it has already been given by God the highest possible dignity—He has ordained it to be the temple of the Holy Spirit. To dishonor the body therefore is to grieve the Holy Spirit, whose temple it is. It is to dishonor the Father, whose noblest creation it is.

The particular form of desecration Paul is warning against is the prostitution of the body in any form of sexual immorality (vv. 13-19). The passions of the body were not meant to be expended indiscriminately and blindly. Rather they were to be channelled into holy living, the building of a Christian home, and the service of God and humanity. These passions belong to God, too, and are reserved to the control and direction of the Holy Spirit. Not a part of us, but the whole of us, has been Blood-bought.

The recognition of the sanctity of the body rules out

[1]Mild obesity is not always proof of gluttony, of course. Sedentary habits combined with a metabolic imbalance may tend toward natural corpulence even when one is self-controlled in eating habits. Therefore not all large people are deserving of criticism. They at least however should seek the advice of a doctor —and follow it!

all forms of self-abuse, of health-destroying vices, of loose exposure to public gaze, of reckless and unnecessary endangering of life, and of mayhem in any form. It certainly includes vulgar joking about the body and its functions.

Yet the Christian needs to avoid the cult of body-worship so prevalent today. There is much emphasis upon the organization of life around the body and its needs, as an end in itself. Some people seem interested in little else but their bodies—clothes, health, cleanliness, rest, care, and medication. The purpose is not to preserve their bodily fitness for better serving the Lord, but for better enjoying themselves. Actually, of course, the world is inconsistent at this point. While it worships the body with the expenditure of countless hours and billions of dollars pampering and coddling it, at the same time it destroys the body by its indulgences and vices. But the Christian will neither treat the body as an end in itself nor abuse the body. He will simply seek to "glorify God" in it.

If so, he will be equally careful to respect the bodies of others. Here a narrow view of the body must be avoided: the term represents not only a physical organism but the *person*. To say that the body is sacred is to say that the person is sacred. This includes *every* person. Skin pigment or economic status or geographic origin cannot diminish or erase this sanctity. Therefore to despise people because of accidental and superficial differences of race and color is to dishonor God, their Creator, just as surely as to despise our own persons.

6. II Tim. 2:15: *Study to shew thyself approved unto God, a workman that needeth not to be ashamed* ... True, this is addressed originally to Timothy as a preacher, but the principle has far wider application. Whatever our calling, we are obligated as Christians to improve ourselves in order to reach maximum usefulness in the kingdom of God. Contentment with medi-

ocrity is unethical because it deprives God and others of the full measure of our powers. "Give of your *best* to the Master," the song says; but really, the word "of" should be omitted. Give your best! The word "study" means, "Do your best" (RSV). A workman who doesn't do his best ought to be ashamed.

Systematic treatises on ethics would have a section called *Duties to Oneself*. Self-improvement is a duty. It embraces the improvement of our emotions, our aesthetic appreciation, our mannerisms and voices, and certainly our minds. But Christian ethics can never rest with a period after "Oneself." Self is not the end. Biblically there is no such thing as a duty to oneself—in complete isolation. Rather, our so-called duties to self are first and last duties to God. We owe it to ourselves to get a good education, to get enough sleep, to improve our tastes, to save for a rainy day, and so forth, *only if we owe these things to God.* Remember, the principles noted in I Cor. 10:31 and 6:20 carry over here. Whatever is not first a duty to God is not really a duty to ourselves. Our prior duty to God may *prevent* us from saving for a rainy day, or going to school as long as we would like. Then we do *not* "owe" it to ourselves to do these things. "For ye are not your own . . ."

It might be well at this point to review the terms of our consecration. In our concept of duty, those terms become exceedingly practical and decisive. We must absolutely stop living as if we belonged to ourselves. We don't even "owe" a *vacation* to ourselves, excepting as we owe it to God as a means of achieving the added effectiveness in His service which a vacation (wisely taken) would achieve. We must never be guilty of violating the rights of others and the honor of God by persuading ourselves that we "owe it to ourselves" to explode in anger, or throw off restraints and obligations in order to find "personal fulfillment." We are living in a day when Christians at times are advised to kick over the traces and "have their fling" as a so-called duty to self. Let us be so thoroughly grounded in this matter that "crackpot" counsellors can never brainwash us into non-Christian conduct.

7. Rom. 13:1: *Let every soul be subject unto the higher powers.* Systematic treatises on ethics would not only discuss our duties to ourselves but *duties to the state,* and all other legitimate authorities. No Christian can know what these duties are without studying carefully Rom. 13:1-7, at least. This passage makes perfectly clear that God's people are to be (1) obedient to properly constituted civil authorities and law officers; (2) careful to observe the law as a matter of principle and conscience, for the sake of the common good; (3) faithful in paying taxes; and (4) courteous and respectful toward all public servants. (5) A further duty is implied, based on the entire Bible—that of involving oneself in civil and community affairs. This would include voting, letter writing, holding office, and other ways as God may lead us.

Abraham Lincoln taught that our liberties could be preserved only by "reverence for law." He had abundant biblical support for his position. Today we think we have improved our philosophy by substituting sentimental concern for the individual, on the assumption that persons are more important than principles. This is a half-truth which we have interpreted as meaning that the liberty of persons must never be shackled by restraint, or that principles should never be enforced. *Away* therefore with principles and laws which impinge upon the private wishes of the individual. But Lincoln had a sounder understanding not only of liberty and law but of human nature itself. As long as men are unholy, their basic liberties will be preserved only by civil law. Only as men obey law can they remain free.

Holiness folk should see this clearly, and live accordingly, whether anyone else does or not. They should therefore conform conscientiously to property regulations, corporation laws, and other known requirements, even though some rules seem to be of doubtful equity. Changes should be sought by agitation, not by flagrant and wanton violation—unless, of course, the law is a direct affront to our known duty to God.

This carefulness should by all means include traffic laws. When state and federal agencies are spending millions to cut down highway slaughter, they should be able to count absolutely on the full cooperation of Christians—and doubly so on Christians who profess to be sanctified wholly. For Christians to treat traffic laws and officers as nuisances to be outwitted, and thus foster in their children and others a lawless spirit, is utterly inexcusable. And for a Christian to attempt to "fix" a ticket for a careless violation is contemptible. It contributes to the very laxity in modern law enforcement which he claims to deplore. These are ethical blind spots which can no longer be tolerated.

Summary

1. When a person becomes a Christian he determines to live right, and adopts the Bible as his rule of conduct. Because the Bible is yet new to him, he will welcome the early guidance of church rules and teachers.

2. When he is filled with the Spirit this purpose is intensified, his sensitivity to right and wrong is sharpened, and he has added power to do what he sees is right. But in some areas he may not yet have clear "light." He must continue therefore to study the Bible, listen to sermons, and read helpful guidebooks that he may eliminate any remaining ethical "blind spot." His goal is to make his outward life perfectly exemplary for the Lord's sake. As a holy person, he is committed to the highest ethical standard he knows, therefore he is careful and conscientious.

3. In determining what is right, love for God and man will be his guiding principle. This will be a "second mile" sort of love, which goes beyond the letter of the law. The Christian desires not just to be right enough to stay out of jail and keep one's reputation, but to be redemptive—to show Christ in his business dealings and in all other personal relationships.

4. Certain verses of Scripture should be memorized as constant reminders of the structuring principles of Christian conduct. Only by seeking to practice these principles can we maintain a good conscience. These scriptures are Matt. 7:12; Rom. 13:10a; Rom. 12:17b; I Cor. 10:31; I Cor. 6:20; II Tim. 2:15; and Rom. 13:1.

QUESTIONS FOR DISCUSSION

1. How far should we go in "second mile" ethics, and in providing "things honest" in the other person's sight? To the extent of paying bills which we do not believe to be a legitimate claim upon us?

2. If we are inclined to be "touchy" and sensitive about criticism, would this suggest that we have a real problem at this point? What should we do about it?

3. According to I John 1:7 the continuance of both fellowship and cleansing from sin is dependent on walking "in the light." How would you define "walking in the light"?

4. What are some reasons why the church should provide ethical guidance for its members in the form of rules?

5. In what respects can we properly speak of the "game of life"? Are there parallels between "sports" and the "game of life"? Is there any scriptural support?

6. What did Abraham Lincoln mean by "reverence for law"? How can this preserve liberty?

CHAPTER ELEVEN

The Ethics of Holiness
—Some Problem Areas

Scriptures for background:

Matthew 6; 7; 8; Rom. 14:13-23; I Cor. 8:1-13; 10:14-33; I Thess. 4:1-12; 5:11-24; II Thess. 3:1-15; Eph. 4:25—5:21; Heb. 13:1-8

There are many problem areas in the thinking of holiness people today. A few of these would assume less importance if some who are "holiness" people by profession were a little more holy in reality. When people begin to love this world and its pleasures more than God and His pleasure, they begin to become very nettled by church rules, so-called denominational "immaturity," "legalism," and "pharisaism." They become experts in rationalization and permissiveness, in the name of broad-mindedness. Christians who are intent on making it to heaven, however, will not cultivate the art of balancing precariously on the edge of the precipice, but will want a margin of safety. They therefore will say gratefully (as a church member testified recently): "I need the church rules." Most people do—as *guidance* and as *reinforcement*.

At sea no English ship is covered with insurance unless the "Plimsoll line" is visible. This is the line painted on the hull marking the safe-load limit. Wise shipowners will keep it well out of the water. Church rules can be thought of as sort of a "Plimsoll line." When the soul is overloaded with liberties and the rules ignored, it will sink in the next storm. But this is the negative side—that which concerns watchfulness against peril. On the positive side, those who are cultivating the spiritual life and serving God as enthusiastically as *holy* people should be doing will not feel "cramped" in life. They will be so happily busy that they will have no sense of loss or restriction. They are not the ones who are muttering in self-pity, and casting envious and longing glances across the fence.

Nevertheless, there are current social problems which involve us as "perfect love" believers, about which some serious thinking should be done. We should study the Bible carefully to see what are the practical implications of perfect love toward other classes and races. Is there evidence of unintentional cliquishness and class consciousness in our churches? How can this be avoided? There is also the problem of employer-employee relations, and the even more delicate problem of the ethical and Christian use of one's surplus. The industry and thrift of holy living will tend toward business success and the accumulation of a surplus. If not handled according to biblical principles of *stewardship*, this surplus will prove to be fatal to the spiritual life.

In fact, holiness folk should be concerned about more than just being right themselves. They must have an active interest in the many social issues which concern public morals and human welfare. Among these are good citizenship, law enforcement, poverty and hunger, oppression and exploitation, automation, population explosion, rehabilitation, the care of the elderly (the number of whom has already "exploded"), alcoholism, drug and tobacco addiction, pornographic literature, juvenile delinquency and crime, the abuse of public media of communication and entertainment, Sabbath desecration, marriage and divorce. Whatever affects people for good or ill is inherently of interest to sanctified Christians.

Because of limitations of space, we will confine our attention to two sticky areas, vital to the maintenance of spiritual health: the necessity (1) of sanctifying our personal liberties, and (2) of protecting the sanctity of sex. Afterward we will summarize the whole scope of holiness ethics by the affirmation of some basic guidelines.

Personal Liberty Versus Christian Example

Mutable morality. There is an area of ethics which has sometimes been called "mutable morality." Simply put, this term refers to changing standards of right and wrong. Some standards, of course, are unchanging; they are as eternal as God, their Author. We are not concerned here about these but rather about the many things which are only relatively wrong—things not actually harmful in themselves. By the word "relatively" we mean that the rightfulness or wrongness of some practices must be determined in the light of their relation to other considerations. Among these factors are the culture or age in which we live, the associations in the public mind concerning the issue, the maturity or immaturity of the participant. Some activities may not be intrinsically harmful but only potentially harmful. Such would be the case if they became *too important* to us, or if they stole time and strength from more valuable activities, or if in some way they were a real stumbling block to others.

Some Christians lack "light" concerning the wrongness of certain things, and so still do them, innocently. On the other hand there are those who are unaware of the *rightness* of certain things which they should be doing. As standards on dress, eating and drinking, and forms of recreation vary greatly from age to age and country to country, so will practice vary, even among equally godly people. A mark of maturity is the ability to distinguish between essentials and nonessentials. Basic modesty, temperance, decency, healthfulness, and wholesomeness should be sought by God's people everywhere. But it is expecting too much to suppose that they will be exactly uniform in the application of these criteria to the details of everyday living.

The Apostle Paul discussed thoroughly this whole problem in Rom. 14:13-23; I Cor. 8:1-13; and I Cor. 10:14-33. The particular question which took most of his attention was whether or not Christians should eat meat which had been offered to idols in the practice of idolatry. Paul insisted that the meat wasn't hurt any; it was as nourishing as any. And the idols were a fiction anyway. Therefore, when invited out Christians should not ask prying questions but eat what was set before them with thanksgiving. But they should avoid eating it if the host raised the issue, lest it appear to him that they were participating in idolatry. The classic statement of the love which subordinates personal rights to the welfare of others is: "Wherefore if meat make my brother to offend, I will eat no meat so long as the world standeth" (I Cor. 8:13). While the Christian is not a slave to public opinion, he is everlastingly concerned about his *influence*.

"Weak" and "strong." In respect to these matters Paul makes the distinction between "weak" Christians and "strong." The weak Christian tends to be overly scrupulous about matters which in themselves are of little consequence. But he is sincere in his scruples;

therefore for him to violate these will bring him into darkness. The Christian who laughs at the weak brother for his scruples may become responsible for his downfall. The "strong" Christian is the more mature, better informed believer whose knowledge of God and the Scriptures gives to him a more accurate evaluation of these petty issues.

But perfect love puts into this "strong" Christian something far more important than superior knowledge. It gives him *concern*. Therefore he is less anxious about his liberties than he is about his influence. He is willing to forego some places, some practices, and some possessions, if the full exercise of his rights would lead another whose conscience was not ready for such liberty to copy him.

Older Christians possess a responsibility toward new converts to guide them into paths which are safe and on which they will become strong and steady. They must be especially careful not to lead them into paths on which they might lose their way. The proper question for the Christian to ask is not whether this or that will harm *him* but whether his indulgence will harm *others*.

Keep in mind that we are now thinking only of practices which in themselves may be perfectly harmless. Their peril is mainly psychological (but indirectly spiritual), because of their evil associations or questionable character. Take "playing cards," for instance. One might argue that "paper is paper," and if there is no gambling, what difference does it make what kind of funny designs are printed on the paper as long as only a simple, innocent game is being played? But there are spiritual and moral overtones created by the history of some things that cannot be easily removed. The emotional and mental associations surrounding playing cards are so impregnated with evil that many Christians, saved from a life of sin, could not safely handle them, no matter how innocent the game. To do so would bring serious danger to their souls. For this reason there is only one charitable course for all Christians to take: "If card-playing make my brother to offend, I will touch no cards so long as the world stands." And the church doesn't.

But Paul is not discussing vices which are harmful in themselves, such as gambling, liquor, or tobacco. A man might be a Christian temporarily and still use tobacco, if light on the matter were completely absent. But this is a totally different matter. In this case it is not a question of being *weak* or *strong,* as if a *weak* Christian should avoid tobacco but a strong Christian could use it. It is rather a question of obedience to light. When knowledge comes, one must quit smoking or backslide. In this area of ethics there is no place to talk about a strong Christian having "liberties" which weaker Christians don't have. To avoid the vices for a while, then begin them in the name of broad-mindedness is not the progress of spiritual growth but the regress of a backsliding heart. Therefore a Christian avoids dancing, tobacco, liquor, gambling, and such practices, not only because practicing them would be detrimental to one's influence, but because they would be detrimental to one's own soul. They are wrong in themselves because they are inherently harmful.

But let us not stray from the main principle, which is that love must draw the lines. Nowhere will this be more meaningfully done than when personal liberties are sacrificed for the good of others. For the sake of his influence, a truly sanctified man would in his ethics rather be fussy than fuzzy.

Love but not bondage. While restricting one's personal liberty (and the ability thus to restrict oneself is the highest liberty of all) for the sake of others, one must be careful not to get into *bondage* to others. This occurs when one blindly tries to bow to every other person's conscience. There must be a discerning whether its sensitivity is sincere and vital, or merely censorious and crotchety.

Some Christians are weak and would really be *harmed* by my liberty. Others would not be harmed by my liberty, only annoyed. They are self-appointed policemen whose time is spent spying out the liberty of their fellows on trifling issues that might offend personal *taste* and private *notions* but have nothing to do with the subversion of morals.

One woman, for instance, told a conscientious young Christian that a sanctified woman would not wear red, whereupon the sensitive Christian promptly burned her new forty-dollar coat. She was to be commended for manifesting the *spirit* that is essential to perfect love—a willingness to sacrifice personal desires for the sake of others. In this she was strong, not weak. But she lacked *wisdom*, for she failed to discern between a petty quibble raised by a Pharisee, and a vital issue over which a weak Christian might stumble into sin. The decent covering of one's body is a vital issue; the choice of color in one's coat is merely a question of personal taste.[1]

From legalistic Pharisees who would exact unscriptural and artificial requirements, Paul admonishes that we stand "fast therefore in the liberty wherewith Christ hath made us free" (Gal. 5:1). But it is even more important to keep free from moral looseness, compromise, and carelessness. As Paul stated it: ". . . only use not liberty for an occasion to the flesh, but by love serve one another" (Gal. 5:13). Let us restrain our liberty for the sake of the weak. At the same time let us protect our liberty from the chains of the legalist. But in all cases let us "by love serve one another."[2]

---

[1] At least this is the case in our present culture. It might conceivably be morally significant in some other cultures.

[2] This section is taken from an article by the author which previously appeared in the *Herald of Holiness*.

Woman's supreme role. The Bible teaches that God created woman as a helpmeet for man. Men and women therefore are intended to live as companions and mutual aids in the service of God and on the journey to heaven. They are intended to complement, check and balance, strengthen and encourage each other. Their role as mutually supporting companions through life and mutually helpful partners in the achievement of successful probation takes precedence over all other purposes in their relationship. This is not the secondary but the supreme meaning of sex. The fulfillment of this purpose is the primary goal of marriage, and its success makes a successful marriage.

But this function can be fulfilled even by the unmarried. A noble, pure, Christian woman is an inspiration and stabilizing force to all men with whom she associates, whether she is married or not. Jesus was grateful for the help of the women who composed an important segment of His party (Matt. 27:55). Paul, too, frequently expressed his gratitude and debt to women (Phil. 4:3; etc.).[3] But, in turn, Jesus and Paul, though unmarried, were a blessing to the women with whom they associated. Every Christian man, whether married or single, has an obligation to every woman he meets, to be the kind of person that will strengthen her, and inspire the best in her. Each has a contribution to make to the other.

The first thing holiness does is to restore this spiritual concept of the function of sex to primacy. Even when married, a woman's supreme purpose is not to bear children, or to satisfy sexually either herself or her husband. It is to help her husband to be the kind of man

---

[3]Paul was unmarried, at least during the period of his Christian ministry (I Cor. 7:8).

he ought to be and to get to heaven. If she bears children, her supreme goal as a mother must be to bring them up in "the nurture and admonition of the Lord," that they may be finally saved. No lesser goal is worthy of Christian motherhood.

This Christian view of marriage rescues it from the animal laboratory, where it is seen purely as a biological affair. The first step in achieving complete mastery of the physical aspects of sex is to see that they are only of relative and subordinate importance. Physical fulfillment in sexual relations is not the supreme value and purpose in life, nor is this fulfillment absolutely essential to rich and useful living. And in every sanctified heart there is a determination to fulfill the higher spiritual function without either compromising or tarnishing it. For this reason the relationship in holiness churches between men and women is generally happy and healthy. This will be true always to the extent that the members of the church are genuinely sanctified wholly.

Home and family. However the Bible also places very high value on the home as the basic unit of society. God has ordained, according to the clear teaching of the Scripture, that the reproduction of the race be accomplished exclusively by and within the husband-wife family unit. The Bible also recognizes that, to achieve this purpose, God not only made man and woman mutually attractive and helpful, but planted within their nature the urge to mate, not seasonally and temporarily as animals do, but with one partner for life. "For this cause shall a man leave his father and mother, and shall cleave unto his wife; and they twain shall be one flesh" (Mark 10:7; see also Gen. 2:24; Matt. 19:5; Eph. 5:31). Within the context of marriage the full expression of the sex instinct is not sinful, nor is it low and vulgar. It is a sacred gift of God intended to enrich and bless.

But actually the Bible emphasis is not so much on romantic love as the basis for mating as it is on the marriage bond itself. The Bible would not countenance for one moment the modern notion that love is the only all-important requisite, and that legal marriage is secondary. No matter how intense and fervent and "sincere" it may seem to be, erotic love is sinful in God's sight if it is not in harmony with His clearly prescribed laws. Sex outside of God's laws always results in someone being hurt. And while the marriage relation, when kept holy, contributes to man's happiness, nothing can cause more degradation and misery than the perversion and desecration of this relation. This means any perversion at all, at any level. And no sin more swiftly brings the wrath and sure judgment of God. "Marriage is honourable in all, and the bed undefiled; but whoremongers and adulterers God will judge" (Heb. 13:4).

The Christian's commitment. It is essential, therefore, that a Christian understand fully God's intentions concerning sex and be completely committed to this holy standard. It is also mandatory for the wholly sanctified believer to understand that holiness has not unsexed him or in any way made him immune to the subtle pressures of this life force. Sex cannot therefore be ignored by Christians. It must be frankly faced, and compelled to serve the holy life, not defile it. Paul said, "But I keep under my body, and bring it into subjection: lest when I have preached to others, I myself should be a castaway" (I Cor. 9:27).

Unfortunately a vast and growing number of people see sex as the most important ingredient in their happiness. They are therefore determined to have it at all costs, even if it means breaking vows and homes, to say nothing of divine laws. Single people, deprived of marriage, engage in clandestine affairs, believing that they "owe it to themselves" to experience life "to the full." But sound conversion and sanctification decisively dethrone sex, and enthrone Christ. Holy people still have a natural interest in sex, but not a morbid, obsessive interest. They will use the gift if God allows, but not abuse it. If God withholds it, they will not snatch at it frantically, nor permit themselves to sink into lifelong self-pity and anxiety. A wholly sanctified person is determined to rule his sex desires, not let them rule him. His hope of success lies in the fact that his chief interest is elsewhere. He loves Jesus Christ and desires to please Him more than self. This holy drive gives him the motive power to accept partial or total denial of his sex nature rather than satisfy himself at the expense of the kingdom of God and the honor of Jesus Christ.

Why mastery may not be easy. But even holy people may not find complete mastery easy. This is true for several reasons. One lies in the nature of the sex drive. At its highest level it has a spiritual quality which develops into affection and romantic love, capable of high and lofty self-sacrifice and devotion. But it also has a simple, elementary biological side, which is just as purely physiological as digesting a piece of pie. This physical side consists of plain, unvarnished sex urges which are created by glandular and organic activity. As such they are spontaneous and irrational—and *amoral.* That is, they are as morally "color-blind" as one's saliva glands which may function, when one is hungry, at the mere sight of food. To the extent that men and women are controlled by these spontaneous but powerful urges which arise from the body chemistry they are living on an animal level. But to the extent that these impulses and desires are ruled by divine law and divine love is true manhood and womenhood reached. True love will itself dictate the control of sex impulses.

This ideal is difficult for depraved man, whose love is marred by selfishness and whose entire nature is "loaded" in the direction of animal passion. But it is the standard lived resolutely by the Christian. However, though God gives grace to regulate sex within the context of holy love, this divine grace—even **sanctifying grace**—does not change our bodies or "deep-freeze" their glandular processes. Therefore the holy person may still feel the sex urge whether married or unmarried, and at improper times as well as proper. Naturally this urge will give rise to thoughts of a sexual nature. Or the reverse process may occur: thoughts of sex suggested from *without* may give rise to the bodily response, for the body and mind are constantly interacting. The thought thus created (either from without or within) is not sinful; it is natural and inevitable. If the thought concerns only the legitimate means of satisfaction, it is not even a "thought of evil." But even a true "thought of evil" need not become an *evil thought* if we reject it at once with decisiveness. Mature, strong Christians have not only learned to repudiate a wrong impulse or thought at once, but have cultivated an *aversion*. The result is that both the rejection and the repugnance become like reflex actions. This is the highest possible moral stability. Sex in itself has a strong pleasurable appeal; no normal person feels repugnance toward it naturally. Our souls must be trained to feel repugnance toward the wrong use of sex without attaching the same repugnance to the right use of sex. This is the mark of developed Christian character.

There may be occasions during times of illness and glandular disturbance when the sex urge will be abnormally strong and will consume more attention than is desirable. This may be caused not only by the state of one's health but by either the training or habits of the past. But normally the sex urge will find its proper balance in response to a period of disciplined living, with the dominant interest of our lives spiritual rather than earthy. If an excessive degree of sensitivity and unruliness persists, one should consult a physician. If there is found to be no chemistry imbalance, then the only answer is more prayer plus more discipline in one's total living. Above all, there should be more active involvement in positive, wholesome activities.

Married people will find victory through the power of divine love shed abroad in their hearts by the Holy Spirit. This divine love turns a husband or wife into an unselfish and spiritually minded partner who is more concerned about his companion's happiness than his own, and more concerned about everyone's eternal spiritual welfare than about earthly pleasure. This gives grace to quit demanding ideal happiness for oneself. As a result, adjustment, self-denial, and consideration become possible as the tone of life—and a cheerful tone at that. This *agape* love, plus love for God, completely rules out unfaithfulness, regardless of the provocation. The affections will not be permitted to stray to someone else who promises to give more happiness to ourselves. For it is not happiness we are concerned about so much as holiness. We want above all things to honor God and help our loved ones. Therefore we will go not only the second mile, but the third and fourth—and the thousandth—as long as the Spirit shows us that the last mile may prove redemptive. Even when both partners are sanctified, there will be rough spots, due to native incompatibilities and unavoidable misunderstandings, but sanctified partners will be *determined to make it*. And they will, by God's grace—to their everlasting enrichment.

Problems of the unmarried. Single people professing heart holiness have problems peculiar to their situation. It is easier for them to appropriate special grace to control the desires of nature if they believe God has called them to remain in the single state. This may be because of a specific task for which God has chosen them. But this, if successful, will not be a merely negative fight. It will be a positive, active, full, creative life in which they find a substitute fulfillment and thus a large degree of happiness. There are hundreds of such Spirit-filled single people who waste no emotional energy feeling sorry for themselves. Psychologists call this sublimation.

The modern approach is to speak of emotional security in wedlock and sexual fulfillment as a "need" of human personality. The assumption often is that emotional and mental health is impossible without it. The next logical step is: "If I need it as a sick person needs medicine, then I owe it to myself to take it! If such is the case it can't be wrong—the wrong would be in depriving myself of it." This is the slippery logic of many people.

So we must take another look at the word "need." Paul said, "It is good for a man not to touch a woman." He is simply saying: "Don't be afraid—celibacy won't hurt you." It is not an absolute or indispensable need in the sense that air, water, and food are. A man or woman can be perfectly healthy, both mentally and physically, without sex fulfillment. This sensible attitude of independence is far more wholesome than the morbid complex that thinks the need for sex is on the same plane as the need for sleep. The trouble is, our oversexed culture has oversold us on sex. We have been made to believe we must have its satisfaction or we will develop all sorts of neuroses and complexes. But this is a bluff of our sex-mad world, which Christian single folk need to "call" with high courage and resolution.

Reasonable safeguards. So great is a sanctified person's love for Christ and His holiness that he cultivates a healthy fear of all forms of uncleanness and immorality. If this is genuinely his frame of mind, he will be careful to observe reasonable safeguards. And he will cheerfully cooperate when in certain group situations those safeguards are imposed on him by the rules of the group or institution.

Such safeguards surely include gentlemanly and womanly conduct at all times toward the opposite sex. At this point Satan has tripped some "holiness" people. They have supposed that holiness put them beyond temptation and therefore have assumed a liberty which gave to the devil perfect material for a trap. This does not usually follow the path of conscious sex urge as such, but takes the way of tender affection, sympathy, solicitude, then emotional entanglement. But somewhere along the path will be the *trap*. Satan knows just where to put it and when to spring it, with disastrous consequences for time and eternity.

Modest dress, too, is an indispensable safeguard. A Christian woman is completely out of character when she follows slavishly the world's extremes in fashion—in any direction. It is inconceivable that a *sanctified* woman could have in her heart a desire to be a "fashion plate" so as to call attention unduly to herself. Nor would she dress daringly and immodestly when to do so is to contribute to the sex looseness of this age.

Of course there is nothing wrong with the body! But there is plenty wrong with the hearts of men and women. Therefore God intends that the body shall be decently covered to encourage virtue and discourage vice. Women should aim to dress in such a way as to enhance their feminine charm as Christian women, filled with the Holy Spirit, not as women of the world. If this is their aim they will study to avoid extremes of either showiness or dowdiness. They will so dress that attention is attracted to them as persons, not just as bodies.

For everyone, married and single, men and women, a healthy attitude toward sex is essential. That attitude can be summarized as follows:

1. **Sex** in its physical expression is important, but not all-important. It is not absolutely indispensable for health, happiness, or usefulness. Sex in all of its aspects

is holy when conformed to God's will, sinful when selfish and lawless.

2. The body is not sinful but sacred. It is the temple of the Holy Spirit. "Therefore bring glory to God in your body" (I Cor. 6:20, Phillips). But if we are to glorify God in the body, it must be kept *clean, clothed,* and *consecrated.*

3. Within marriage, the privileges of the home are sacred and are to be accepted with thanksgiving. They are not to be soiled by sex obsession and intemperance, or by selfishness and lack of consideration.

4. Apart from marriage the supreme mission of woman can still be fulfilled—to be a helpmeet to man in the work of God. Every woman can find a place where she is needed.

5. If single persons—men or women—are so constituted that the deprivation of their state needles and nags excessively, they can take consolation in knowing that, though they may not be entirely happy, they can be entirely holy. In the long run they will find the joys of holiness infinitely more satisfying and enduring than the pleasures of the body would ever be.

6. Two of the basic differences between carnal persons and ones wholly sanctified concerning the above fact are that: (1) the latter *believe* this, while the former doubt it; and (2) the latter are willing to pay any price to have God's will in their lives, while the former secretly feel that the price is too much. "For Demas hath forsaken me, having loved this present world" (II Tim. 4:10).

Summary

Three questions should be asked when seeking to determine the rightness or wrongness of a practice: (1) What is the ultimate influence or effect of this action on those about me? (2) Upon society at large? (3) Upon myself? If these questions are honestly asked against the background of the scriptural guidelines which we have been studying in these two chapters, we will arrive at some definite criteria:

1. *Whatever undermines the home is wrong.* And anything does which weakens moral resistance, which leads to jealousy and quarreling, to unfaithfulness, and to divorce.

2. *Whatever undermines the Church is wrong.* This makes Sabbath observance an ethical obligation, even apart from the fourth commandment.

3. *Whatever undermines the state is wrong.* Good citizenship is "part and parcel" of holiness ethics.

4. *Whatever exploits human weakness for gain is wrong.* This condemns the tobacco, liquor, and gambling empires, the deliberate purpose of which is to extend these practices in the interests of more and more profits.

5. *Whatever oppresses, degrades, despises, or exploits human personality is wrong.* This condemns racial oppression and likewise unjust labor exploitation.

6. *Whatever arouses the beast in man rather than the noble is wrong.* This principle will rule out a large percentage of modern fiction and TV entertainment.

7. *Whatever coarsens human relations and cheapens life is wrong.* Human relations which are refined and considerate should be fostered, and a high regard for human life cultivated. This brings into question also personal foolhardiness, or anything which would deface, defile, or expose to unnecessary peril the human body.

8. *Whatever enslaves the will, stultifies the soul, weakens the body, or dulls the mind is wrong.* It is a violation of the principle of stewardship. This principle would indict modern vices, as No. 4 would indict the syndicates and industries which promote them.

Questions for Discussion

1. What is meant by the statement, "Our character is revealed not so much by our professions as by our preferences"? Is this true?

2. What is meant by the "collective conscience of the church"? What weight should this carry in determining one's personal practices?

3. How is the Christian principle of love-structured liberty related to the use of alcoholic beverages?

4. How do prize fighting and Sunday sports rate when examined in the light of Principles 2, 6, 7 of the "Summary"?

5. How can "legalism" be distinguished from proper Christian conscientiousness?

6. What are some things pronounced right (or indifferent) by modern society which the Bible pronounces wrong?

7. Will democracy endure without high moral standards and a high level of self-discipline on the part of the citizenry? Why?

8. Will perfect love tend to soften natural incompatibilities between married partners? How?

CHAPTER TWELVE

Turning Temptation into Triumph

Scriptures for background:
    Gen. 3:1-10; Matt. 4:1-11; Luke 22:39-46; I Cor. 10: 1-15; Jas. 1:1-15.

"How can a holy heart be tempted?" is a perennial question. The reasoning back of the question is that if all evil desires were purged, and we loved God fully, there could be nothing in us that the temptation could take hold of, nothing that could respond favorably to a suggestion to do evil. Would not any favorable response at all prove the presence of evil desire? And if there is no desire in the heart sufficiently sympathetic to this particular temptation to spark any interest whatsoever, then no real temptation, as such, is felt. What passes for temptation is only a mental suggestion.

Obviously the suggestion to steal a car would not be a real temptation to a holy person. The idea would probably never enter his mind unless someone else put it there. Even then his spontaneous reply would be,

"Don't be crazy." And if a person *feels* no urge to wrongdoing can he properly be said to be tempted? He may be enticed by others, but is the enticement necessarily a temptation? Therefore the original question is seen to be legitimate—and difficult. A further question is: If a sanctified person can experience genuine temptation, in the sense that he feels an urge to wrongdoing, *when* and *how* does a mere suggestion become a real temptation?

The first step in seeking an answer is to examine the nature of temptation.

THE NATURE OF TEMPTATION

Temptation and trials. The most important passage on this subject is Jas. 1:2-15. The King James Version leaves us puzzled because in verse 2 temptation seems to be a good thing, while in verses 12-15 it is an evil thing which God has nothing to do with. More recent versions, however, clear up the difficulty by translating the Greek word in verses 2 and 12 as "trial" and in verses 13-14 as "temptation." A trial is an unpleasant experience which tests our faith and purpose. God's aim in trials is to strengthen us ("the testing of your faith produces steadfastness," says the Revised Standard Version). But a temptation is a direct enticement to do evil. Its aim is to persuade us to sin, thus bringing about, not our strengthening, but our weakening and final destruction. ("Sin, when it is finished, bringeth forth death.")

Certainly the two may exchange places. A temptation is also a trial, inasmuch as it tests the strength of one's love for God, and one's moral resistance. Likewise a trial may turn into a temptation, inasmuch as we may be tempted, in the midst of our trial, to sin against God by doubting Him or rebelling. In this way Job's trial became a severe temptation.

Temptation and desire. In the account of Job, the part Satan plays in both trials and temptations is plain.

But in the passage from James the devil is not mentioned once. "But every man is tempted when he is drawn away of his own lust, and enticed" (v. 14). Evidently a big part of temptation comes from inside of us. How can this be, if we are purged from sin, and love that which is good and hate that which is evil?

A missionary bought a much-needed new hat one day, but paid considerably more than she intended. When her husband mildly remonstrated by saying, "Why didn't you say, 'Get thee behind me Satan'?" she replied, "I did, and he said it looked just as good from the back as it did from the front!" This playful answer was the confession, of course, that in this case the devil could not be blamed; the culprit was her own strong desire for the hat. "Strong desire" is what the Bible means by "lust." Two things must be nailed down solidly right here: *A true temptation is not possible unless there is some strong desire within us for it to take hold of.* For example, it was when Jesus was extremely hungry, having fasted forty days, that Satan suggested the turning of stones into bread. But the second is equally as fundamental: *A strong desire is not necessarily evil just because it is temptable!* Jesus' desire for food was not sinful, nor was His great, passionate desire to be accepted by His own people. Nor was His yearning to rule the kingdoms of the world.

The word "lust" then, is misleading, for it leaves the impression that only people with *evil* desires can be tempted, whereas in fact holy people with holy desires can be tempted too.

Now let us return to the missionary and her hat. We must say two more things about her shopping spree. We must confess that, although the anecdote illustrates our proneness to blame the devil when we should frankly pin the blame on our own desires, it poorly illustrates temptation. Buying the hat, even paying a little more than intended, was not necessarily wrong. Unless she could testify that she distinctly felt a check of the Spirit and deliberately overrode it, we would not be right in accusing her of sin. God allows us considerable latitude in such personal matters.[1] This is mentioned not only to get the missionary "off the hook" but to encourage some extremely sensitive Christians who are forever feeling condemned at this point. They feel whipped for having yielded to their desires here and there, when their problem may only be a finicky conscience over trifles.

But since we have started to talk about the lady, we may as well go on to the second observation: Regardless of the strength of her desire, she couldn't have yielded to it if there hadn't been a hat for sale. Which helps us to see the further basic element in temptation: *not only must there be desire on the inside but there must be opportunity or enticement on the outside.* I might have a strong desire to go to Mars, but one could hardly call this a *temptation* to go to Mars, inasmuch as at present there is no opportunity. It is only when an opportunity is presented that one can be "drawn away" by desire. Desire is set aquiver by the sight of its object. It is drawn toward it as filings to a magnet.[2]

But the desire, of itself, to go to Mars is not sinful (though its wisdom might be debatable). Nor would *going* to Mars necessarily be sinful if safe means of interplanetary travel were available. Then how can this be an example of *temptation* for a holy man? Simply because he might have a conviction that going to Mars was not God's will for him at this time! On this basis, the

---

[1] A *pattern* of persistent and habitual extravagance or excessive clothes-consciousness would soon be checked by the Spirit—but that is a different situation.

[2] Of course in respect to some sins a person can create his own "opportunity" in his imagination, and thus become guilty in the sight of God (cf. Matt. 5:28). But at the moment we are not considering this aspect.

desire to go to a neighboring city or country might be a temptation, and yielding might be a sin. Therefore no matter how innocent is the desire, and how innocent the object (in itself), the holy man, if he would remain holy, must pause long enough to refer the desire to Higher Authority. This is the meaning of keeping life under the constant and immediate supervision of the Holy Spirit. And while the Spirit may give us a lot of leeway in the purchase of hats, He has very definite plans for us in major matters.

Temptation and sin. Sin is not simply yielding to desire. We yield to desires every day without sinning, climaxing with the extra strong desire at the end of the day to get off our feet and get into bed. It is only when the satisfaction of the desire is seen to be out of God's will that the desire is a temptation pulling toward sin. There are these basic factors to notice here:

1. The person must see that yielding to the desire would be out of God's will. The conscience flashes a red light; the Spirit restrains. If the Christian is totally unaware that any moral issue is involved—if he feels no check and experiences no uneasiness of conscience—and proceeds to act in complete innocence, he is not guilty of sin at all. This is true even if later he discovers that he acted unwisely.

2. If he senses that yielding will be sin, he is at once in the throes of a moral decision. He can avoid sin only by a swift and final decision in favor of righteousness, no matter how painful is the denial of desire. Up to this point there is no sin. How long the soul can tremble on the brink without becoming guilty only God knows— but not very long. For if he begins to debate, trying to find excuses for what he knows is wrong, he has already compromised. "Whatsoever is not of faith is sin" (Rom. 14:23). His will has already yielded to a degree. He may yet recover himself and turn from the evil, and pray,

"Lord, forgive me for being so weak." But generally when we parley with temptation, knowing it to be such, we soon yield completely. In any case, it is when the will unites with the desire that sin is conceived, and "sin, when it is finished, bringeth forth death" (Jas. 1:15).

But the temptation itself involves no sin as long as it is uncompromisingly resisted, no matter how intensely we feel its hot breath. Furthermore, the emotion of desire, even when decisively denied, does not always subside at once. But it will subside *if we don't prolong the battle by secretly feeding it.* But if we do we stand guilty.

The advantage of a Christian who is wholly sanctified is that the supreme battle between God's will and self-will has already been fought and won. That issue is settled once and for all. If we remain Spirit-filled we face every day and every new experience in this deep-down frame of mind. Therefore any subsequent struggle is relatively short-lived. Emotions may be moved, but not the purpose to obey God. It is easier to surrender the passing when one is passionately attached to the permanent.

How then can a sanctified person ever be in danger of falling? How can he be tempted in such a way that he will yield, and commit sin?

How the Pure Are Tempted

The psychology of desire. Desire is a wish for something to which our minds attach value. Whether we desire baubles or the true gold in life depends on our value-system. This in turn depends on one's total concept of the meaning and purpose of life. A true Christian naturally tends to have a very intelligent value system because (1) he *looks ahead.* He distinguishes the transient from the enduring, and says with Jim Elliot, "He is no fool who gives up what he cannot keep in exchange for what he cannot lose." (2) He *looks beneath* the surface and thus distinguishes seeming value from real. He is not captivated by the superficial glitter of life but seeks the solid, satisfying virtues of integrity and honor. (3) He *looks up* and thus distinguishes between earth and God as a proper value-base. He is therefore not deceived by earth's standards of value but tests all by the Creator himself. He can say with Livingstone, "I shall place no value on anything I have or possess save in relation to the kingdom of our Lord Jesus Christ."

Thus the Christian is not easily fooled by false values. But the *possibility* is always present, because there is an additional factor in this question of one's value-system which may cause trouble. It is the simple fact that a "value" is *seen as such because it is believed to be a source of pleasure.* Our desire reaches for this pleasure. Now notice:

1. God has created an order of life in which normal functions and activities (ideally, at least) are pleasurable.

2. God has created us with a natural liking for pleasure and dislike of pain. The reverse of this we recognize as abnormal.

3. God has created a universe in which pleasure is the rightful and normal fellow of righteousness, while pain is the normal and rightful fellow of unrighteousness. The Scriptures say, "The way of transgressors is hard," and, "He that soweth to his flesh shall of the flesh reap corruption; but he that soweth to the Spirit shall of the Spirit reap life everlasting," and, "To be carnally minded is death; but to be spiritually minded is life and peace." These are the laws of life, written in the very nature of the universe.

4. But God has permitted Satan to juggle life just enough to make it seem that holiness and pain belong

together, while sin and pleasure belong together. Thus temptation becomes possible. When Satan persuaded Eve not to fear the forbidden fruit, and she saw that it was "pleasant" and "good," she ate with excitement. She probably enjoyed it—for a brief time. It *did* taste good—in her mouth. And so there is pleasure in sin. It is this anticipated pleasure which sparks desire, which in turn makes temptation possible. If Eve had looked at the tree and had seen it as *ugly* and the fruit *bitter,* she would have seen nothing desirable in it. With nothing pleasurable involved, the "temptation" would have had no force.

The desires of the sanctified. But our aim is to apply this to the sanctified believer particularly. He still has a normal preference for pleasure over pain. It is when the will of God asks him to deliberately reject beckoning pleasure and choose looming pain that temptation is possible. For example, being human, we prefer eating to fasting; therefore we are tempted to feast rather than fast. We prefer approval to disapproval; therefore we are tempted to seek approval, and to shrink from those things which will bring disapproval upon us. No matter how thoroughly sanctified, no Christian is going to "enjoy" taking a stand that is sure to bring down on his head the wrath of the boss, or his friends, or his family. Here is where pastors can be tempted to compromise just enough to keep the goodwill of everybody.

We prefer to be attractive rather than repelling. No Christian who has good sense and breeding as well as good religion would particularly enjoy being called "an old hag" or an "oddball." He might bear it sweetly, but it would hurt. If he were being persecuted for Jesus' sake he could rejoice, by divine grace. But this would be possible only if the epithets were prompted by his religion, not by his appearance. No, this desire to be acceptable in polite society, and a thousand and one other desires, are as natural as breathing. But every one is a hazard, for it has in it potential temptation—to satisfy it by illicit or worldly means.

Our Lord in the garden. But we can go right to the heart of our wonderful Lord to see the sharpest suffering in temptation that has been experienced on this earth. Very reverently let us listen to His anguished prayer when His sweat was as it were great drops of blood: "If it be possible, let this cup pass from me: nevertheless not as I will, but as thou wilt" (Matt. 36:39). To try to understand what the "cup" was is not necessary at the moment. We need only to see that here was a holy Man, spotlessly, impeccably sinless, who was saying, "Not my will, but Thy will." Here was a confession that the two wills might not entirely agree. The prayer implies that if the Father's will were done the Son's will might not be. *My* will, Jesus is saying, is to avoid the cup. But even as He passionately prays He senses that the Father's will is that He drink it.

How truly human as well as holy was Jesus here! He was still conscious of himself as an individual. As an individual He not only had strong preferences, desires, and aversions, but He was fully aware of them. He did not deny them or hide them. He expressed them in "strong crying and tears" (Heb. 5:7). He too shrank from pain and craved pleasure. But lest we misunderstand and thereby cheapen our Lord, we must hasten to add that it was not merely the choice between physical pain and physical pleasure which wrenched His sensitive, pure soul that night. It was the spiritual torture of feeling sin's defilement, of tasting the horror of condemnation, and even worse, of being identified in death with corrupt, lost humanity. His soul was trembling as a wounded bird thrown mercilessly to the wild dogs, or as a lost child crying as in a nightmare for his father's strong arms when the arms are not there. There is no suffering like that experienced by a pure soul when shadowed by sin, or that of a loving, obedient son when estranged from his father. And so we are compelled to speak of the cup after all. It was not just the bare experience of dying, but of dying with that blackness and loneliness of becoming a "curse" for lost men.[3]

And what was the pleasure so exquisite that the very thought of its deprivation meant unbearable pain? It was that delight more transparent in its purity and more rapturous in its intensity than any other joy possible in human experience: perfect oneness with God. This for Jesus was the one absolute value; therefore its loss, even for a brief hour, would mean the absolute extremity of suffering. Now, in facing the Cross, Jesus *desired* with strong desire to cling to this pleasure and avoid this pain. It was this struggle with His desire—the holiest desire which man may ever experience—which we call His temptation in the garden.

What was the secret of His victory? It was the fact that this holy desire was subordinate to another desire equally holy but even stronger: to obey His Father! His deepest will was for *His* "will" to be overruled by God's will. Beneath His human, personal desire was the yet deeper desire that His Father be honored. And this desire to honor His Father was stronger than His desire to avoid the pain. Therefore He was able to speak that crucial word, "Nevertheless . . ." "Father, no matter what My will is, Thy will must rule. No matter what My desires are, Thy desires for me I choose, at whatever cost of anguish to myself." This is that perfect love which has the last word. Its last word is always the right word, because it is the kind of love which enslaves all desire.

We need to be reminded that this is a pattern for us.

[3]See H. Orton Wiley, *Epistle to the Hebrews* (Kansas City: Beacon Hill Press, 1959), pp. 183-84.

This is the explanation of our temptations, and this is the secret of our victory.

We still have natural preferences and natural aversions. And surely it is true that we are coarser and earthier than was our Lord. We have many different desires pulling in different directions. But if we are truly sanctified there is one master desire which corrals and chastens all others—that is to please God. There is one supreme pleasure which excites us and captivates us more than all others—the sheer delight of His presence. Nothing means more than to have His smile, to follow His way, to do His work, obey His Word, and be in His will. Our natural desires on secondary issues may constitute temptations, but the real strength or weakness of the temptation will be determined by the strength or weakness of our love for God. If we can say, "I'd rather have Jesus than anything," *and mean it,* the devil will be hard put to trip us up. If our deepest joys are in Christ, not in people; in heaven, not in earth; in spiritual pleasures rather than sensual, then we are well-nigh invulnerable. But if our relish for holy things loses its zest, and spiritual joys lose their luster and begin to seem tame and insipid, we are on shaky ground. Almost any trifling pleasure trumped up by the devil will turn our heads and send us tripping back to the attractions of Egypt.

One more point needs to be added here. Our Lord's strong desire to escape the cup was basically a passionate desire not to forfeit for one moment the pleasure of His Father's smile. At the very point of His holiest desire was His mightiest temptation. But He saw through the ironic deceptiveness of the situation, just as three years previously He had, in the wilderness, seen through the stratagem of the devil. He knew that if His desire for unbroken pleasure with the Father was demanded at the cost of the *will* of the Father, He would lose the pleasure of the Father's smile *anyway.* In that case, however, it would be by His own sin, rather than merely by becoming a Sin Offering in man's behalf. And that would be far worse. Better by far to experience the brief torture of cosmic loneliness than displease the Father. Better to let the hills echo the piercing cry, "My God, my God, why hast thou forsaken me?" than to interpose the wish of His shrinking soul in place of God's will.

Our deepest temptations *can* come at the point of our holiest desires. We desire to win souls—and we are bedfast. We long to preach the unsearchable riches of Christ—and we are laid on the shelf. We want to draw close to God—and God seems to hide himself. We wish we could take the Good News to those who have never heard—and we are bound by the chains of preventing circumstances. Our desires can be drawn out toward good things—even the highest—as well as evil. Strange as it may seem, our holiest desires can become our darkest Gethsemanes.

When a group was visiting the supposed Garden of Gethsemane outside of Jerusalem, a young man whose face had become increasingly drawn and ashen suddenly flung himself prone on a huge rock in the garden, his body racked with convulsive sobs. He had been called to preach and was studying in a Middle East Bible school. But he also had fallen in love with a beautiful Christian girl and the two wanted to get married. To finish his schooling, and preach long enough to save a bit, would take years. Then had come an offer from the United States Army to work for them as a mechanic at $8.00 a day. They could be married at once! But it would be at the cost of his education and his call. No wonder he was stretched prone on the rock! He knew in that moment the "fellowship of his sufferings" as he too said, "Nevertheless not my will, but thine, be done."

Is it not apparent that love is the key? Love for God

dulls all other lures and breaks the spell of every other passion. On our part, perfect and intense love for God is an invulnerable armor against the enemy. On the enemy's part, any hope of success must be by a strategy which aims at two goals: (1) the weakening of our love for God, and (2) the camouflaging of the evil, making it appear good. Against the second, a constant study of the Bible, a sensitive conscience, and the Holy Spirit, *honored daily in His supervisory role*, are sufficient safeguards. Against the first, our safeguard is found in looking constantly "unto Jesus the author and finisher of our faith" (Heb. 12:2). This looking must include a frequent *turning* to Him in prayer, a joyful *trusting* of Him as the Lord (Rom. 8:28-39), and a humble *taking* from His Spirit and His Word both strength and direction.

In this direction is *growth unlimited* "in grace, and in the knowledge of our Lord and Saviour Jesus Christ. To him be glory both now and for ever. Amen" (II Pet. 3:18).

Summary

1. A real temptation is an urge to commit sin. It thus differs from a trial, although a trial may become a temptation to doubt or rebel.

2. Temptation occurs when a desire is drawn toward its satisfaction. This may be presented either as a real-life opportunity or as a synthetic opportunity in our imagination.

3. Desires are not necessarily sinful in themselves but they may become the occasion for temptation. Good desires may be enticed to satisfactions contrary to God's will.

4. Temptation of itself is not sin, nor an evidence of a sinful heart. A tendency, however, to play with temptation is a mark of sinfulness.

5. Sin is involved when the will concedes to the enticement, either mentally or overtly.

6. If Christians should yield to temptation and commit sin, they need not despair, for the same divine mercy which forgave them once will do so again, if they are truly repentant (I John 1:9; 2:1-2).

7. But to presume on this mercy by willful repetitions is to callous and ultimately damn the soul.

8. One's natural preference for pleasure and shrinking from pain may cause some difficult duties or experiences to become temptations, even after one is sanctified wholly.

9. As with our Lord, even our holiest desires must know their Gethsemane. "Not my will, but thine, be done."

10. The pleasures of sin will not be able to recapture our attention if we keep before us the beauty of Jesus and the joys of righteousness. Our hearts must respond to the glad affirmation of the Psalmist: "Thou wilt shew me the path of life: in thy presence is fulness of joy; at thy right hand there are pleasures for evermore" (Ps. 16:11). *Only in perfect love is there safety.* The intensity of our devotion to Christ will be the measure of our strength to resist temptation and to withstand trial.

Questions for Discussion

1. What is meant by the clause in the Lord's Prayer which says, "And lead us not into temptation . . ." (Matt. 6:13)?

2. What are some of the ways by which modern Christians can expose themselves unnecessarily to temptation?

3. Is the genuineness of our love for God indicated by our hatred of and distaste for everything that is unclean and unchristian?

4. What is our responsibility in building up within ourselves resistance to the allurement of evil? How can this be done?

5. Can growth in grace be gauged by the increase of our skill in negotiating the trials and temptations of life?

For Further Reading

BALDWIN, H. A. *Holiness and the Human Element.* Kansas City: Beacon Hill Press, 1919. 2nd ed., 3rd printing, 1953. 110 pp.

CATTELL, EVERETT LEWIS. *The Spirit of Holiness.* Grand Rapids, Mich.: William B. Eerdmans Publishing Company, 1963. 103 pp.

CHADWICK, SAMUEL. *The Way to Pentecost.* Berne, Indiana: Light and Hope Publications, 1937. 128 pp.

CHAPMAN, JAMES B. *The Terminology of Holiness.* Kansas City: Beacon Hill Press, 1947. 112 pp.

COOK, THOMAS. *New Testament Holiness.* Ft. Washington, Pa.: Christian Literature Crusade, 1963. 158 pp.

CORLETT, D. SHELBY. *Lord of All.* Kansas City: Beacon Hill Press, 1962. 117 pp.

CORLETT, L. T. *Holiness, the Harmonizing Experience.* Kansas City: Beacon Hill Press, 1951. 94 pp.

DU BOIS, LAURISTON J. *Guidelines for Conduct.* Kansas City: Beacon Hill Press, 1965. 87 pp.

GISH, DELBERT R. *Practical Problems of the Christian Life.* Kansas City: Beacon Hill Press, 1964. 88 pp.

HARPER, A. F. *Holiness and High Country.* Kansas City: Beacon Hill Press, 1965. 376 pp.

JOY, DONALD M. *The Holy Spirit and You.* Nashville: Abingdon Press, 1965. 160 pp.

PURKISER, W. T. *Conflicting Concepts of Holiness.* Kansas City: Beacon Hill Press, 1953. 110 pp.

———. *Sanctification and Its Synonyms.* Kansas City: Beacon Hill Press, 1961. 96 pp.

SMITH, MAJOR ALLISTER. *The Ideal of Perfection.* London: Oliphants Ltd., 163. 127 pp.

SMITH, HANNAH WHITALL. *The Christian's Secret of a Happy Life.* Westwood, New Jersey: Fleming H. Revell Company, 1952. 248 pp.

STEELE, DANIEL. *Hints for Holy Living.* Kansas City: Beacon Hill Press, 1959. 80 pp.

TAYLOR, J. PAUL. *Holiness—the Finished Foundation.* Winona Lake, Indiana: Light and Life Press, 1963. 216 pp.

TAYLOR, RICHARD S. *The Disciplined Life.* Kansas City: Beacon Hill Press, 1962. 108 pp.

For Deeper Study

ANDERSON, T. M., Editor. *Our Holy Faith—Studies in Wesleyan Theology.* Kansas City: Beacon Hill Press (printed for Asbury College), 1965. 347 pp.

GEIGER, KENNETH E., Compiler. *The Word and the Doctrine.* Kansas City: Beacon Hill Press, 1965. 429 pp.

PURKISER, W. T., Editor. *Exploring Our Christian Faith.* Kansas City: Beacon Hill Press, 1960. 615 pp.

TURNER, GEORGE ALLEN. *The Vision Which Transforms.* Kansas City: Beacon Hill Press, 1965. 348 pp.

WILEY, H. ORTON. *Christian Theology,* Vol. II. Kansas City: Beacon Hill Press, 1941. 517 pp.